SECRETS OF
THE 800+ CLUB

SECRETS OF THE 800+ CLUB

How to Raise Your Credit Score,
Maintain Good Credit, and
Live the Life of Unicorns

Terrell Dinkins

Alpharetta, GA

ISBN: 978-1-63183-877-4 - Paperback
eISBN: 978-1-63183-878-1 - ePub
eISBN: 978-1-63183-879-8 - mobi

Library of Congress Control Number: 2020915375

Printed in the United States of America   090420

♾ This paper meets the requirements of ANSI/NISO Z39.48-1992 (Permanence of Paper)

Cover Design by Asifat Kunle

To Mr. David Coggins, my high school impact teacher.
Thank you for helping me land my first job, analyzing credit reports.
So many future lessons learned from that first job . . .
Rest in peace.

Those who don't know the secrets pay the highest price.

—Terrell Dinkins

Contents

Acknowledgments

I would like to thank God for allowing me to walk in my purpose and find my voice. Sharing my experience and knowledge about personal finance and wealth-building are two of the reasons why I am on this earth. Nothing can hold me back from sharing what I know. To whom much is given, much will be required (Luke 12:48, KJV). If we have been blessed with knowledge, talents, wealth, time, and the like, it is expected that we benefit others with our gifts. It is almost a disrespect to God if we don't give to others.

To those in the social media community who openly share stories of how they have been held back because of credit issues, I thank you for giving me fuel. Those who don't know how pay the highest price. It's time you learn how to take control of your credit. Lack of credit knowledge has cost you too much for far too long.

I will always be grateful to my friend Sonia Booker, who gave me the courage to write about what I know. It was with her encouragement that I wrote my first book, *One Bucket at a Time: A Woman's Guide to Creating Wealth*. She told me years ago I had a book in me and people need to hear my message. Cheers, Sonia— here's to book number two!

Jeff Dinkins, you continue to support me in all of my entrepreneurial endeavors. Thanks for keeping me grounded and showing me a different perspective to all of my curiosity.

Jeffrey and Jordan, I am amazed at how you've grown and now see the importance of my work. Thank you for being my cheerleaders. Jordan, I appreciate you telling me to focus on my book, and Jeffrey, thank you for reminding me of my many talents and pushing me to use them.

Introduction

Many people receive good advice, but only a few profit from it.

There's a story behind every story, and my narrative is no exception. A few years ago, I received an invitation to attend a Wealth and Wine event at an upscale beer and wine superstore in Atlanta. I accepted the invitation for two reasons: I was curious about the setup of the wine tasting at a local store (a possible concept for a future event of my own), and I am always open to learning something new on wealth-building. Honestly, I could almost guess the concept, but still, I wanted to see if the host had something new to say that I had not already heard.

I arrived at the event and was surprised to see the beverage store had a quaint setup in the back perfect for the occasion of a presentation and wine tasting. The host of the event was pretty thorough in his introduction, and the material presented was what I expected. The young man discussed adding insurance as an asset class to your existing portfolio. I had no issue with the concepts presented. I had heard it all before. To my surprise, there was a second host who was a real estate agent. She came to the front of the room and gave us some interesting facts about the real estate market in Atlanta and how our city was one of the hardest hit during the 2008 real estate crash. Her goal as a real estate agent was to make as many people happy as possible by helping them get a piece of the American Dream by owning a home. One of the biggest hurdles, according to her, was getting a credit score high enough to purchase a home with a decent interest rate. One of my favorite takeaways from her presentation, and I now use the phrase, was, "Your credit score determines the type of mail that comes to your mailbox." I was moved and on board with everything she was saying, until she hit us with "The Sales Pitch"! It was her sales pitch that motivated me to write this book.

Before I hit you with her pitch, I find it necessary to share how disheartened I am with the wealth gap we have in this country. And the credit score is one of the contributing factors to this gap. Having poor credit also limits access to capital, which can help create wealth. Two of the main ways wealth is created in this country is through the stock market and real estate. The real estate agent was correct and poignant with her assessment of the credit score. Those three-digit numbers not only determine the type of mail that comes to our boxes, but it also determines the price we pay for our homes and cars, and even whether we receive a loan if we want to start a business.

Your credit score has become your bartering tool. So if that is the determining factor in whether this real estate agent sells a house that will benefit her and the client, why was she pitching to her clients, and the audience that night, a credit repair program? Not only was she in the business of selling houses, but she was also in the business of selling the credit steps to get you in the house. "For a one-time setup fee ranging from $175 to $225 and a monthly investment of $125, for which you must commit to for one year, we can help you clean up your credit and raise your credit score," according to her slides. This pitch and countless others have become big business. People are taking advantage of others' misfortune and lack of knowledge when it comes to figuring out how to raise a credit score. The world knows how significant those three digits are. Some people are so desperate to clean up their credit they are willing to pay big bucks to have a fresh slate. In reality, raising your credit score is something you can do on your own, and it doesn't have to cost you $175 or any monthly fee.

Honestly, I don't have an issue with anyone charging for their time if they are providing a legitimate service. I do take issue with a person's ill intentions in the service they are selling. I had a problem with her saying you could do this in your spare time to make extra money. Her approach was MLM (multilevel marketing) at its best! She was trying to grow her team, and she had an audience that evening of potential new candidates. The larger her group, the more money she made. She didn't seem to care much about the problem so many Americans are having with their credit. She seemed more excited about the possibility of adding another person to her team. Everybody nowadays has a hustle, and I guess selling credit repair packages was hers. The disturbing thing about the entire situation was the woman never shared her credit score or how she has benefited from her program. She could have had a credit score of 400. No one asked, and she didn't share.

After the little "sales pitch," I walked out of the wine-tasting room, purchased my favorite bottle of wine, and thought long and hard about what I witnessed at the event on my drive home. If I have resolved to walk in my purpose and help others, I can figure out how to help people raise their credit score without it costing them a deposit of $175 and a $1,500 annual commitment. I have an 800+ credit score, and it didn't cost me anything. In fact, having a credit score over 800 has saved me so much money. Having a low credit score causes you to live an expensive life! I have never been denied a loan, and people treat me a bit different whenever I try to make a large purchase. Last year, after driving my SUV for more than ten years and clocking over 280,000 miles, I decided to put her out to pasture and purchase a new car. I pulled up my FICO credit score (at that time it was 834) and called the credit union to see what rates they offered their best credit customers. I took that information to the car dealership and negotiated my interest rate. The first interest rate the dealer provided me was much higher than the credit union rate. When he found out the interest rate I was offered from the credit union, I received a lower offer. My credit score gave me negotiating power and leverage. I had a choice of getting a loan with my credit union or the car dealer's lender.

My 800+ credit score gives me reliable negotiating power and privileges so many people don't have. I've never received a no when it comes to applying for personal credit. I've enjoyed the smiles and nods experienced when applying for credit. My goal with this book is to share with you how to raise your credit score and keep your credit score up once you've built it so you, too, can share these same experiences and more. There is a difference between repairing your credit and raising your credit score. Most people don't have repair issues (they think they do, but don't), such as delinquency, garnishment of wages (via a public record), and charge-off, to name a few. They are stuck with a low credit score and can't figure out how to raise it to the next level. For those who have erroneous items on their credit report, there is nothing magical a credit repair company can do that you can't do on your own. There's no magic bullet. You have to be willing to put in a little work. You will appreciate the outcome when you've worked to get what you want.

Knowing how credit works gives everyone the opportunity to even the playing field. I want to show you how to play in the game. Membership in the club comes with privileges, and I would love for you to become a member. Join me and others who have unlocked the secrets of the 800+ credit score club!

NOTES

_____

_____

_____

_____

_____

_____

_____

_____

_____

_____

_____

_____

_____

_____

_____

_____

_____

_____

_____

_____

_____

Chapter 1
Know Where You Are

You are the captain of your ship. You control the steering wheel. Go where your heart leads you.

Before you can navigate your destination, you need to know your current location. You need a starting point. When it comes to changing your credit score, you need to find out your current number before you can mindfully raise your score. If you don't know your score, you are not alone. Many people are in the dark when it comes to knowing their credit score or how the score is derived. In a survey conducted by MoneyTips, nearly 30 percent of people admitted to not knowing their credit score.

People who are members of the 800+ credit score club started developing credit pretty early. I got my first credit card when I was in college. When I applied for the card, I had no idea about my credit score, but I knew I wanted to create credit. Plus, I thought it would be cool, like most students, to walk around with a credit card. I'm telling my age, but when I was in college, we didn't have debit cards with credit card logos on them. We used ATM cards (which I still carry because they are safer than a debit card).

Before the 2009 Credit CARD Act, credit card offers were given out like candy on many college campuses. My university was no exception. I was able to apply for a credit card without a cosigner.

You still don't necessarily need a cosigner, but giving out the cards like candy is no longer the norm on college campuses. Those days are long gone. Now, it is more challenging to get a credit card. I'll address in more detail later how to apply for credit if you haven't established any yet.

Student Loans and Your Credit

While I am on the subject of college and credit, let's talk about student loans and the impact they have on your credit and future lifestyle. Our country is in a crisis when it comes to student debt. In the United States, student loan debt has risen to over $1.5 trillion, only second to mortgage debt (Statista, 2019). The average monthly student loan payment is $393 and the average student loan debt at graduation is $37,172. Students need to understand that making the decision to carelessly sign for a student loan can haunt them for decades. The loans aren't meant to furnish your wardrobe for a semester. Signing on the dotted line has consequences.

Many college graduates gleefully enter the working world excited about what lies ahead, looking forward to purchasing their first home and making their mark in the workforce and society. Little do they know, the student loan they have placed in deferment could have a considerable impact on their lifestyle and their credit score.

I was scrolling through my social media feed one day and ran across a random question that caught my attention. The question asked was, "What are the biggest financial regrets you have ever made?" Overwhelmingly the answer was taking out a student loan. This was not a scientific study, but a random sample of college-educated adults who are now working and having to pay back the loan. What I have found is parents are not having crucial conversations with their children about debt in general, and yes, a student loan is a debt. Before their children head off to college (or better yet, while they're still in high school), parents should have personal finance conversations with their soon-to-be high school grads. One young lady shared with me that her mother told her they would worry about the loan later. Wrong answer! Now, years after graduating from a private institution, she has over $100,000 in student loan debt. Perhaps the parents and child can take a personal finance course together before heading off to college.

Most students do not have parents who have saved for their child's college education or received an inheritance from a relative (at least, not many in my circle). It wasn't until 1996 that the 529 College plan came on the scene that allowed contributions to grow tax-free as long as the funds were used for education (this plan has changed quite a bit since 1996). Even though there are many options for funding college (grants, scholarships, loans, gifts), the 529 plan being one of them, student loans are still the easiest option for many students entering college. The colleges make it easy for students to apply. Many just waltz down to the campus financial aid office and apply for one, not giving future consequences much thought. Reality sets in when the college graduate gets their first student loan statement. Suddenly, it isn't so cool to have attended your favorite college on your list.

I had to face reality when I graduated from high school. I wanted to attend an HBCU (Historically Black College and University). My heart was set on one particular school, but the math did not work in my favor. I had to face the music that I simply could not afford the first school on my wish list of colleges. Even at the age of eighteen, I knew I didn't want to graduate from college with a ton of student loan debt. Since I was a first-generation college graduate, I didn't get much guidance from home, but I did have a high school counselor who helped me narrow down my decision. I worked throughout high school and saved most of my money because I knew my mother didn't have money to send me away to school. My decision for college came down to dollars and cents. I looked at my college acceptance options and said no to the other three schools on my list, and yes to a local state school with the cheapest price tag. I have no regrets.

When I graduated from college, my loan balance was a little over $1,700, which I paid off pretty fast. I purchased my first car when I graduated from college (no cosigner), and I purchased my first home in my midtwenties. I had the credit to make the major purchases early on in my life with very little debt blocking me. I was able to get a head start because I had practically no student loan debt when I graduated from college.

This should be the goal for every parent and student. It starts with a plan and perhaps making some tough choices—like not attending the first school on your list. Your plan should also include how the debt, if any, will be paid off and when. How long do you want to carry Sallie Mae on your back?

Here's my advice on the subject:

- Parents, talk to your child about the impact of student loan debt. Have the "money talk" with them.
- Students, look at high school as your ticket for college. Make the best grades possible and seek out scholarships early.
- Consider dual enrollment in high school, which gives you college credit.
- Consider junior or community college for the first two years, then transfer your credits to a university.
- Take a gap year to figure out what you want to do in life instead of wasting a loan to figure it out.

- Apply for scholarships (so many organizations give away money for just about anything).
- Look into the military reserve.
- Pay as you go.
- Look at state schools versus private institutions, who don't have the funding for scholarships.

Student loans, coupled with other debt, could have a crippling effect on your credit score. Because so many factors are at stake, you need to know your starting point. I'll dive a bit deeper into discussing student loan debt and credit in chapter 5. It's a passion project for me because so many people avoid this subject, and it's not discussed in families before taking out student loans.

Finding Out Your Score

Finding out your credit score is an easy task. Most credit card companies and many banking institutions offer a free credit score reading. I've been a customer for one large banking institution since college. As soon as I log in to my account, the credit score menu is in full view. The great thing about the score that my bank offers (for free) is it is a FICO score. The FICO score is the most widely used credit score—used in over 90 percent of all lending decisions. The basic FICO scores range from 300 to 850, while industry-specific FICO scores have a broader range, from 250 to 900.

I know I threw you for a loop when I said industry-specific scores. The car, housing, and credit card industries all use different scores to determine whether they want to lend you money or grant you access to credit. On top of all of this confusion, you have different industry scores across all three of the major credit bureaus: Experian, TransUnion, and Equifax. For the sake of simplicity and to keep your eyelids open, I will keep all references of a FICO score to the general risk level and not industry-specific scores. What I have found is your score will not vary much from bureau to bureau and from industry to industry. When I applied for a car loan, for example, my score was only slightly higher than my general credit score.

FICO has changed its scoring method over the years. The most recent version is the FICO Score 9. What's different and better about the FICO Score 9? Specifically, medical collections on your report are treated more favorably, your rental history can be a positive factor in your score, and paid-off collections no longer have a negative impact.

All of the different credit-scoring methods can be confusing, so you don't need to worry about them if you don't know your score. First things first!

Go to www.annualcreditreport.com and obtain a copy of your report from all three credit-reporting agencies. This site is the only free government-approved and authorized site. The bureaus are required to give consumers access to one free report annually as part of the reform to the Fair Credit Reporting Act (FCRA). The FACTA amendment added to FCRA in 2003 gives individuals rights to know what is in their credit report, and that right is for free! Although you have free access to your credit report, most of the bureaus charge you for access to your score.

So for the first exercise in this book, I want you to pull your credit for free using the annual report link and pay for your score from all three of the bureaus. THIS WILL BE THE ONLY TIME YOU SHOULD PAY FOR YOUR SCORE!

If your bank offers you a free FICO 9 score, like my bank, re-trieve that score. Finally, I want you to subscribe to Credit Karma. Credit Karma, a company founded in 2007 and based out of San Francisco, offers you a free VantageScore 3.0 (another scoring model similar to FICO 9). The VantageScore 3.0 uses data from

TransUnion and Equifax (two of the three credit-reporting agencies) and turns the information into a score.

Once you've retrieved your scores from the bank (FICO Score 9), Credit Karma (VantageScore 3.0), and the bureaus, you can compare the scores. You will likely find that all of the scores are pretty close and only differ by a few points. Please note, your credit score is a current snapshot of your credit, similar to a balance sheet of your assets. Depending on when your credit is reported to agencies, the numbers may vary. That's why it is important to review all of the reports just mentioned and see if the information listed is the same. Once you have made a thorough comparison of the reports, select one you will regularly use to keep up with your credit score.

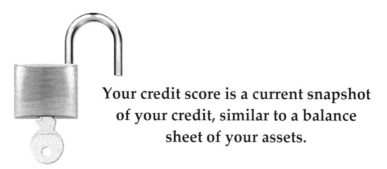

Your credit score is a current snapshot of your credit, similar to a balance sheet of your assets.

Buyers Beware: If you were wondering, Credit Karma is a legitimate credit-scoring company. They do not sell your data but are paid through advertisers of their site. However, do not be tempted to apply to the offers you see on the site. Credit Karma will flash offers in front of you that may be a good fit based on the data in your credit profile. They get paid when you give in to temptation and apply to one of the advertised offers. Just resist and utilize the free information. I'll talk later how applying for credit can be a blessing and a curse!

ACTION STEPS

1. Apply for your free credit reports at www.annual creditreport.com.

    Goal Date _____ Actual Date _____

2. Pay to get a copy of your credit score from all three of the bureaus (Experian, TransUnion, and Equifax). Only do this once for a comparison of other free methods.

    Goal Date _____ Actual Date _____

    > A. Equifax Score: _____
    > B. TransUnion Score: _____
    > C. Experian Score: _____

3. If your bank offers a free FICO Score 9, pull that score and record it!

    Goal Date _____ Actual Date _____

    What is your free FICO score from your banking institution? _____

4.   Apply to Credit Karma (www.creditkarma.com).

Goal Date _____ Actual Date _____

   A.   TransUnion Score (from Credit Karma):

   _____

   B.   Equifax Score (from Credit Karma):

   _____

   Now that you have taken the first steps in getting your baseline scores, you have a starting point. The only way to take your score now is up!

Chapter 2
Cash Won't Cut It!

Cash may be king, but having excellent credit is leverage.

You may have heard of the phrase "Cash is king." It was made popular by radio show host and businessman Dave Ramsey. I am a huge fan of many of Dave's books, and I, too, believe it is best to lead a debt-free life. Having credit card debt can keep you awake at night if you don't have a plan to eliminate it. There's a strategy, however, to utilizing credit to your advantage.

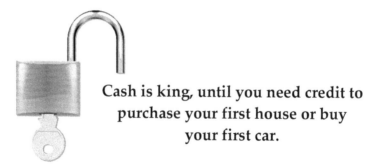

Cash is king, until you need credit to purchase your first house or buy your first car.

Strategic utilization of credit is what I plan on teaching you! Think about this—credit provides you with more purchasing power than cash alone. Cash is king, until you need credit to purchase your first house or buy your first car. Suddenly, cash doesn't look so great and won't cut the mustard if you don't have enough for your purchase. Because we live in a digital age where cash is used less frequently, I think it is a disservice to tell adults they don't need to worry about credit. As an advocate for financial literacy, it should be my duty and others' to teach all adults how to use credit responsibly.

So, let's add a twist to the popular saying with this: "Cash may be king, but having excellent credit is leverage!" Credit reigns because of its leveraging power.

The definition of leverage is your ability to act or to influence people, events, or decision. Your three-digit credit score stands between you and a yes or no to many of life's pleasures. Your score will even be one of the determining factors in the decision to grant you life insurance (your score ruling from your grave). That's deep! Many people who have money problems or who have filed bankruptcy are suicidal. If an insurance company suspects that is the case with you, why would they consider insuring you? They lose if you commit suicide and you have paid less into the policy than the payout of the death benefit. That's why insurance policies have suicide clauses.

When you have excellent credit, you have better control over your lifestyle and the scenarios that play out in your life. To be honest, it's difficult to live a decent lifestyle without credit. If I had to save cash for all the things I now own, I would probably own less. Let's face it, not many people will wait to save up enough cash to purchase a home, a nice car, or other big-ticket items. If used properly, credit can be a valuable tool to help you meet your goals. That's why it is so vital to understand what credit is, how to manage it, and what you stand to gain in establishing and maintaining good credit.

I have a house full of furniture and other toys purchased using credit. I didn't pay one penny in interest for my home furnishings. I leveraged my credit and purchased everything over time, leaving my money in my investments to grow. I'm sure you've seen stores who offer great incentives for you to furnish your entire home: "No interest for twenty-four months." I took advantage of the offers, and I am sure they were hoping I wouldn't pay off the balance in the twenty-four-month period.

> **Buyers Beware:** If you don't pay off the store offers in the time advertised, the interest charges are retroactive. You will pay a hefty interest rate dated back to the original purchase. But, if you play your cards right and pay the bill off during the promotional period, you have what you want and it didn't cost you anything extra (no interest charge). Companies run the promotional offers all the time because most people never pay the bill off in the promotional window. Here's why! The minimum payment showing on the bill is not enough to pay off the entire cost of your purchase during the promotion. When the promotional period ends, you still have a balance and the interest kicks in. Never just pay the minimum balance listed on the bill. Pay more. As a matter of fact, if you have a twenty-four-month promotion, take your balance and divide it by twenty or twenty-two. This assures you the bill will be paid in full before the promotional period ends and you are not stuck paying an astronomical amount of interest on furniture.

Our "personal stuff" makes our lives a bit happier. I used my excellent credit for my purchases and paid the balances off over time. Because of my credit score, the seller didn't charge me any interest!

It's an unrealistic expectation to save cash for everything.

Some people do, but most don't live a cash-only life. There are people who are afraid and do not trust advancements in technology. They are afraid of identity theft, so they prefer using cash for all their purchases. Identity fraud is a legitimate fear. I've had my debit and credit cards hacked. I don't want to scare you, but things happen. Because my debit card was hacked and my banking account was compromised, I no longer carry debit cards. I use my credit card for all my daily transactions. When my credit card was hacked, no harm was done to my personal funds. The credit card company immediately reversed the transaction until they were able to investigate the situation.

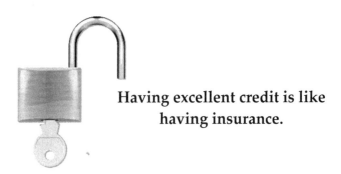

Having excellent credit is like having insurance.

I've been asked if I prefer cash or credit. Let me sum up my answer by saying that having good credit gives you the option to use cash, but having cash doesn't necessarily give you the option to use credit, especially if you don't have credit because you chose to use cash for everything. Having excellent credit is like having insurance. I've had people say, "Well, a 750 credit score is just as good as an 800+ credit score." That's like comparing an A+ average to a 90 average with the goal of keeping an A. There's no room for failure. If you have an 800+ credit score, your score can drop fifty points and you will still receive great rates on credit. If you have a 750 credit score and your score drops 50 points, you are no longer considered an excellent borrower. Being a member of the 800+ credit score club is your insurance policy of always receiving the best! Even if you slip up a bit, you have wiggle room and will never miss out on the privileges of club members.

Using my credit card for all of my transactions provides me with a few advantages:

- Every retailer accepts credit cards, so there is no need to carry cash.
- My personal money is safe when I use credit versus cash.
- Carrying a credit card is convenient, especially if I make a purchase and I don't have enough cash on me.
- There are perks associated with using the card (points).
- Utilization and repayment of the purchases on the card makes me a responsible consumer in the eyes of creditors.
- I can have my personal money working for me and not tied up in a purchase.
- Using my credit card provides me with leverage, especially if I pay the card off in full and stop using it for a while. Credit card companies only make money if I carry a balance (they charge interest on the balance) and I'm swiping the card (merchants are charged a convenience fee for accepting the card). They want you to swipe. When I stop swiping, they don't make money. This gives you room to ask for a lower rate.

As you can see, I am pretty sold on the sheer ease of using credit. I have a long credit history, which has helped push me in the 800+ credit score club. That's why I want you to get started building your credit today!

Having to wait to use cash for all purchases is a delay on life. I purchased my first house at the age of twenty-six. I took out a loan to buy the house (remember, I started building my credit when I was in college) because I didn't want to wait until I had the cash to buy the house. I would still be waiting if that were the case. Needless to say, when I sold the house five years later, I was able to walk away with a nice little profit, which was used to put down on another home.

Let's take a quick review on credit basics.

What Is Credit?

Credit is your ability to be a trustworthy borrower. You obtain the goods or services you want now by promising the lender you will pay them back later, with or without interest.

What Are the Benefits of Good Credit?

In addition to the great advantages I mentioned previously, excellent credit (remember, we are trying to join the 800+ club) gives you access to more borrowing options, such as paying for a home, buying a car, or funding your education. Additionally, employers, insurance companies, cell phone carriers, landlords, and more can use your credit when they are making a decision about you.

I have to share a quick story here about insurance companies. I am an insurance broker. I wanted to start selling insurance for another carrier. Granted, I was not buying insurance; I wanted to sell policies for a carrier. After completing and submitting the application to become a broker for the company, I was sent a polite letter stating that I needed to unfreeze my credit for review before I could broker their insurance. Can you believe it? I was selling their products and they wanted to see my credit. Go figure! I had to temporarily unfreeze my credit to give them enough time to take a quick look at my creditworthiness. I will discuss credit freezing and why it is important in chapter 12.

How Does Credit Work?

Lenders and financial institutions extend credit by lending you money at an agreed-upon rate, amount, and payment terms. When you borrow money and pay it back on the agreed terms, you begin to establish a good credit history. Your credit history is a record of all your accounts, your payment history with the accounts, and the details of how you managed the accounts.

Establishing good credit takes time. You want to start the process of creating a credit history the right way. Once you have established credit, there are several ways to raise your score. But if you think just paying your bills on time is the answer, there would not be a reason to write this book and you would have more people in the club! Before we get into how to raise your score, let's examine how credit scores are broken down into their respective score ranges.

Higher FICO Scores Save You Money

Your FICO score is the most widely used of the different credit-scoring systems, so our examples will be based on that score. Having a higher FICO score can help you qualify for better interest rates. Generally speaking, the higher the score, the lower your interest rate. The difference between a 620 FICO score and an 802 FICO score, for example, can be tens of thousands of dollars over the life of a loan.

There are different levels to your score, and banking institutions have credit score standards when it comes to lending. These levels are pretty consistent across institutions. Here's what each range means:

760+, Excellent Credit

You will generally qualify for the best rates available, depending on your debt-to-income ratio and collateral value.

700–759, Good Credit

You typically qualify for credit, but you may not receive the best rates. Your debt-to-income ratio will be considered along with the collateral value.

621–699, Fair Credit

In this range, you are going to have a difficult time obtaining credit, and if you do obtain credit, you are going to pay for it with much higher rates. In this range, I would suggest not even applying for the credit and wait until you get your score up. It will cost you too much money.

620 and Below, Poor Credit

You may have difficulty obtaining unsecured credit. Unsecured credit is credit that does not have collateral tied to it. A credit card is unsecured credit and a car loan is secured credit.

No Credit Score

You may not have built up enough credit to calculate a score, or you've been inactive for some time so a score is not showing up. Having no score means you need to establish credit.

Let's look at how your payments and the amount you pay over the lifetime of a loan can be impacted by your score. Say two different people are borrowing $285,000 on a thirty-year fixed-rate mortgage. One person has a 620 FICO score and the other has an 802 FICO score. Here's how their payments would break down.

30-year fixed-rate mortgage

$285,000 loan principal
620 FICO Score

5.08% APR
$1,544 monthly payment
$270,808 total interest paid

802 FICO Score

3.49% APR
$1,278 monthly payment
$175,148 total interest paid

In this example, the person with an 802 FICO score pays $266 less per month and saves $95,660 over the life of the loan. The interest saved is enough money to purchase an investment property or some other asset that could make you money. Just as I am, you should be blown away by the difference in savings. This example is why I am so passionate about helping you figure this credit score game out on your own. It's almost unfair that some people have to pay so much more than others because of their three digits. Now, if you had the discipline to save up cash for your home, of course you would save money in both scenarios. But let's be realistic, most people don't have the money or the discipline to pull off this task. According to a 2017 Realtors Confidence Index Survey, reported by the National Association of Realtors, 23 percent of US residents pay cash for their homes. This percentage has continued to drop. In March 2019, 21 percent of home sales were in cash, and in March 2020, that percentage was down to 19 percent. That leaves the remaining 75 to 80 percent of us relying on a loan to make the big purchase.

Now, I have a homework assignment for my readers who are thinking about purchasing a house, or anyone who has a house and after looking at the example above is motivated to get their loan refinanced. I know you are probably asking yourself, why is she discussing a home purchase at this juncture in the book? The answer is because your home is typically the largest asset most people will own. That asset will cost you more than any other possession. The cost also includes interest charges, and because of the interest charges associated with your potentially large asset, you want to make sure you are saving as much as you can on every part of the purchase. So, mark this section if you are thinking about purchasing or refinancing your home. Every dollar saved can be used for something else!

ACTION STEPS

1. Pull out your mortgage statement. What is the current rate on your mortgage?

2. Go to bankrate.com and check out mortgage rates for new purchase and refinancing. This is an excellent site to compare mortgage rates.

3. Is your current mortgage interest rate in the ballpark of other rates? Has your banking institution lowered rates since you financed your home?

4. If there is a local credit union in your area, compare the bank rates to the credit union rates. You may find the interest rates are much lower at the credit union, and it would benefit you to have an account with them to take advantage of their lower rates.

5. How much will it cost you to refinance your home? (I think it is important that you check with several lenders first. Some lenders could charge anywhere from 2 to 6 percent of the loan amount in refinancing costs. If

you are lucky, there are some institutions that offer no-closing-cost refinance.)

6. How long will it take you to recoup the cost of refinancing your loan? This is an important question to find out. If you plan on moving in the next couple of years, sometimes it is not worth refinancing your home. If you plan on staying, however, you could save thousands in interest payments.

NOTES

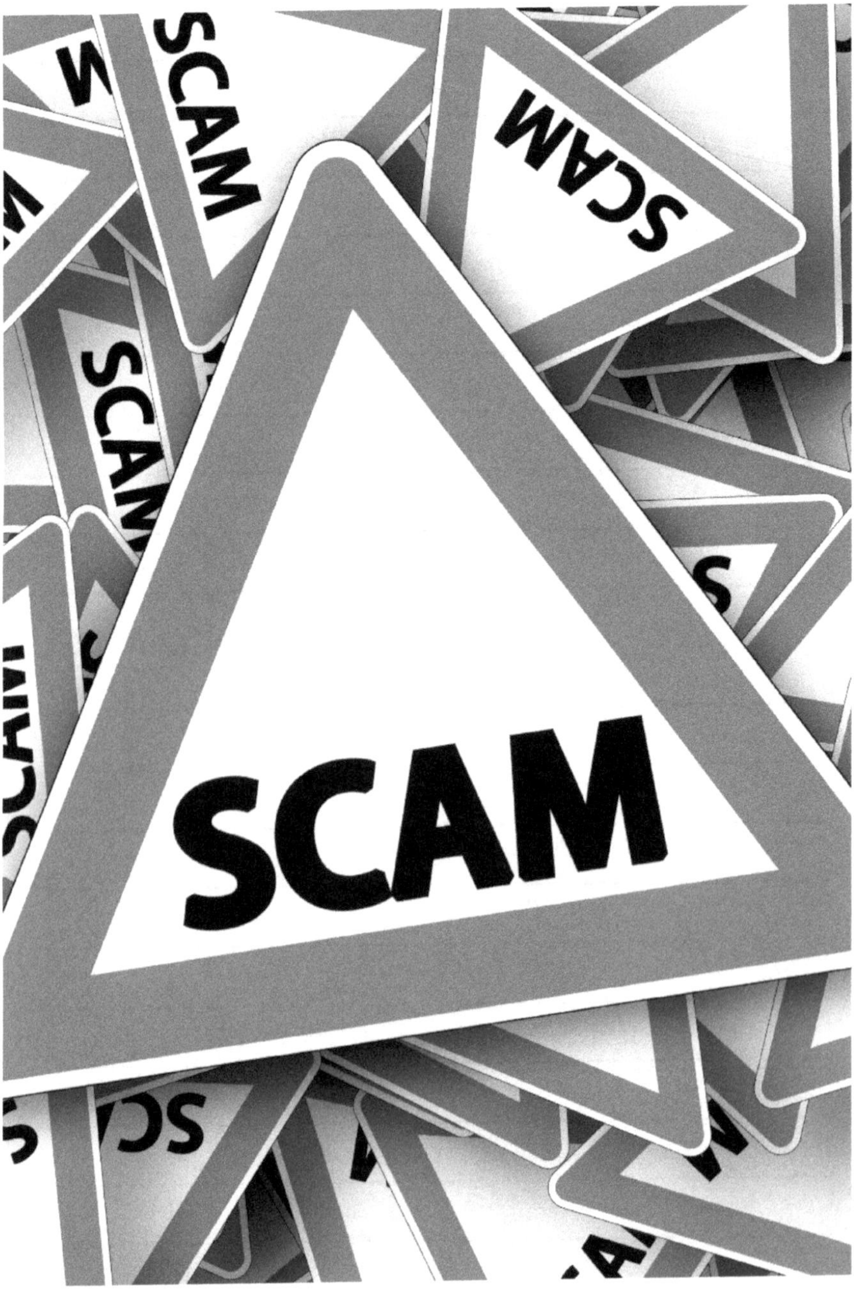
SCAM

Chapter 3

Don't Get Scammed

Money without wisdom diminishes the long-lasting effects of wealth.

I think I've heard every jingle and advertisement promising, "We'll fix your credit—guaranteed!" All the radio and television ads for credit repair are catchy and created so that you will remember them. They lure you into thinking they have the magic formula to make whatever is wrong with your credit disappear— *poof*, your credit is clean! If you are desperate enough to get sucked into the ads, you just might be setting yourself up for an expensive scam that could potentially cost you more in the long run than the fee they are advertising.

Not all companies are scams, and some can actually work on your behalf to help remove erroneous and untimely items off your credit report. The operative word here is erroneous. Legitimate companies shouldn't try disputing items because you one day got out of bed and decided you didn't feel like paying the bill so you want it vanished from your credit. Errors can appear on your credit, and you should have a fair shot at removing them. But there is nothing a legitimate credit repair service can do that you are not capable of doing yourself.

The FTC and Your Rights

The Federal Trade Commission's website has a plethora of information on your rights as a consumer. (The internet is your friend. Look up FTC and consumer rights.) If you are working with a credit repair agency, they must provide you with the following information:

- How much it will cost you to get the results you're seeking
- A written contract detailing the services promised
- A three-day rescission period (you have the right to change your mind)
- Any guarantees
- How long the process will take before you see results

If the agency you are working with doesn't provide you with the above list of rights, you may want to think twice about working with them. Even if they do include the rights in your contract, they could still use a few unscrupulous tactics that might damage your credit even further.

The Scam-Jamming

I know a thing or two about how to get your score to change fast and in a hurry, but it definitely isn't by falling for the scam so many of the illegitimate credit repair companies promise. Have you ever wondered how these companies are able to remove things from your report so quickly? The long-running scam is called jamming. Here's how it works. But before I tell you, don't get any big ideas and think this is something you should try . . . don't, please don't.

The problem with this scheme is it makes it more difficult for the three bureaus (Equifax, Experian, and TransUnion) to keep up and stay on track with legitimate disputes.

What these companies do is send multiple letters disputing items on a person's credit report over and over again whether the information is true or not. This process is called jamming because the illegitimate companies are "jamming or flooding" the system with letters in hopes that the reporting agencies do not respond to one of the letters in time. The goal is to try to get a dispute to fall through the cracks. Under the Fair Credit Reporting Act, a credit-reporting agency must review and respond to every dispute received in thirty days. If the credit repair company is constantly sending the same letter and your credit card company (the data furnisher) doesn't get back to the credit bureau in time (within the thirty-day window), the credit agency is obligated to remove the disputed item from the person's record. So by day thirty-one, if things fall through the cracks, your disputed item vanishes from your report—*poof!* You're happy and think you've gotten your money's worth because your credit report is clean and blemish free.

Here's the problem with valid blemishes removed from your report that genuinely belong to you—the items come back. Lenders report monthly to credit card companies (you can see the report date on your statements). When the lender verifies and reports back the disputed item, the bad debt gets placed back on your credit report. Now, you are back to where you started with less money in your pocket. If credit bureaus suspect the disputes are frivolous in nature, they may refuse to investigate.

You don't have to go very far to find a credit repair company that offers workshops to repair your credit. They are advertised all over the internet, radio, and social media. The prices vary widely. As I mentioned in my introduction, many of the companies make money by growing their teams—multilevel marketing teams. Most multilevel marketing companies focus on distributors rather than what is in the best interest of the customer. The product is not what's driving the sales of the company; recruiting is. Most of the time, no skills are required to do the job. Your main focus is who do you know who wants to make extra money. That money is made by getting people on your team. That's bad business, in my opinion, if I'm a customer who genuinely needs help with my credit and the person I go to seeking help is trying to recruit me into their business. These companies often charge an initial assessment price, then charge an additional price for each negative item you want removed from your report.

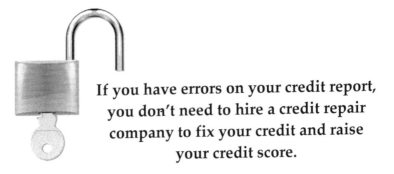

If you have errors on your credit report, you don't need to hire a credit repair company to fix your credit and raise your credit score.

Fix Your Own Credit

If you have errors on your credit report, you don't need to hire a credit repair company to fix your credit and raise your credit score. You can do it yourself and save yourself some money. I'm all about saving a buck if I can. Credit repair companies do not have a magic bullet for removing legitimate false items from your report. There may be situations, however, that warrant hiring an attorney if you have been a victim of identity theft and someone else's debts poured onto your credit report. If that isn't the case, here are a few steps you can take to clean up your credit:

1. First, get your hands on your credit report to see what's on it. You have the right to receive one copy of your report for free once a year from each of the credit bureaus. Go to www.annualcreditreport.com and pull your report from one of the bureaus every four months. For example, order one in January, May, and September so you will be current all year. I would also suggest subscribing to one of my favorite places to keep an eye on my credit: Credit Karma, which will give you free access to your data from TransUnion and Equifax. Since Credit Karma provides free information for TransUnion and Equifax, I would pull the Experian report first from the annual credit report site.

2. Pull out a highlighter and scan your reports for errors and possible identity theft. You know what should be on the report. Make sure the information you see belongs to you. Look at your address (old and new), your name, and your social security number. Make sure it's you. I am one of those people who uses my middle name, so my credit reports reflect all the name combinations I've used over the years to apply for credit. I'm okay with that because I know it's me. Do as I say, not as I've done in the past. One habit you should adapt is to always use the same version of your name when applying for credit. This is something I do now but didn't when I first started applying for credit. Oh, and if you are a junior or a senior, make sure to add it each time you apply for credit as well.

3. Look to see if you have any debts that have surpassed the

statute of limitations, which is usually seven years. If the debts have passed the seven-year mark, you can dispute the items to have them removed from your report. Keep in mind, however, that the statute of limitations for debt-reporting and debt-disputing may be different depending on the state. That's why we have the internet, so you can look it up! If you discover that one of the debts on your report is outside of the collection period, the creditor cannot sue you or threaten to take you to court. If your conscience is eating you up, you can still pay off the old debt, but BE AWARE! There is a possibility that once you start paying on this old debt, the clock could start ticking again on the statute of limitations. The debt collector can then sue you for the debt and start harassing you for the full payment. You could negotiate on the amount to pay. If you do this, be specific and put it in writing, as in, "I will pay you fifty dollars a month and have this cleared up in twenty-four months." You could also try your luck at negotiating pennies on the dollar, even forty to fifty cents on the dollar. Personally speaking, if the statute of limitations has run out, I would let sleeping dogs lie. Don't rock the boat if it's not moving. Get the debt removed and keep it moving.

4. Document, document, document! If you are going to dispute an item on your report, the Federal Trade Commission recommends you send copies of all the documents via certified mail with a return receipt so you have proof your documents reached the agencies. The FTC has a sample dispute letter you can use to dispute items on your report. If you search "FTC sample dispute letter," the example will pop right up.

5. If Lady Luck is on your side and your handiwork

resulted in the negative items being removed from your report, you can ask the credit bureaus for a free copy of your new, correct report. These reports can then be mailed to anyone who denied you credit or employment (within the past two years).

6.   If all your work didn't work in your favor, you can always include your dispute letter in your credit file.

Some people do not want to deal with this process. I know I mentioned illegitimate companies on the prowl to take your money, but there are legitimate nonprofit organizations that will help you for a fair fee. The two that come to mind are Credit.org and NCFF (National Foundation for Credit Counseling). Both organizations are nonprofits designed to improve the financial well-being of individuals and families.

The title of this chapter is Don't Get Scammed! So if it sounds too good to be true and someone is professing to create a miracle with your credit, run. And by all means, don't give them your hard-earned money.

Chapter 4
Your Financial Road Map

Be just as committed to steering your money as you are to achieving your goals.

Life is a journey and we have to live with the consequences we make for ourselves along the way. Sounds cliché, but it's true. So when it comes to our credit, the decision should be made early in life (young adulthood) that having good credit is a good goal to set. Making this decision early on leads to a less bumpy journey. For the most part, we have a choice of how scenic we want our life route to look. Having bad credit out the gate makes it so difficult to dig yourself out later.

Lessons about credit should be taught in high school.

Personally speaking, lessons about credit should be taught in high school. I do not understand why at this point in our country, with the mountain of debt that has been consumed by most American households, we haven't instituted personal finance courses as a mandatory prerequisite for high school graduation. Students are doomed from the start if they have grown up in a household where money was a taboo subject. You have some adults who feel the topic of money is grown folks' business. So, if the children aren't learning healthy life lessons about money at home and it's not taught in schools, most young adults are doomed from the moment they walk across the stage at high school graduation.

After graduation, those same students who were never taught basic personal finance go out and take out a student loan for college, and Mommy and Daddy are no help because many of them sign for the loan and let their kid get a loan too. These are the same parents who are just as lost about money as the kid. The rest of the story is downhill, because it is at this point the debt load starts piling on.

Politicians are pushing their agenda to reduce or forgive student loan debt, but no one has discussed a plan to help people figure out how to prevent the debt crisis in the first place.

Since we are on the subject of student loan debt, let's talk about it. Student loan debt is usually the start of the debt crisis for most households. You graduate from college with debt, then you have to figure out how to live, which usually takes more debt—the new car, the apartment, food, and utilities. I'm sorry to say this, and I'm sure someone will not like what I'm about to say, but it does not make financial sense for someone to come out of undergraduate school with a mountain of student loan debt! There are far too many options. I'm not saying a small loan should not be an option, because it is expected that at least a portion of your college education will be financed with a loan if you don't get a full ride through scholarships. Students and parents should weigh all their options before they sign off on a loan and understand the impact it will have on their life style after graduation when they have to start paying back the loan.

Student loans are a national financial crisis in the US as the second-largest debt category, only trailing mortgage debt. In the first quarter of 2019, student loan debt was approximately $1.52 trillion and steadily climbing. The average student loan debt per person is around $31,000 and the average monthly payment is close to $400 per month. How many stories have you heard of a student taking out a $20,000 loan to cover their first year in college, only to come to the realization that college isn't for them? Money conversations are crucial! We can change the statistics about college debt and the debt of the young adult. First of all, most eighteen-to-twenty-year-olds don't have a clue what they want to do in life. Why waste $20,000 trying to figure it out?

As an African American woman, I would be remiss if I didn't take a moment while I am discussing student loan debt to say that student loan debt is a wealth killer for people of color, especially in the African American community. It's one of the main reasons why there is a huge wealth gap in this country. According to a September 2019 study published by the NAACP (and there are other studies to back this fact), "Student debt is a significant drag on the entire economy as it depresses the purchasing power of millions, preventing people from starting families, investing in their own businesses, going back to school, and buying homes. And because students of color carry larger debt burdens, these consequences also exacerbate the racial wealth divide by impacting families of color the most acutely. Without action, this problem will only worsen."

Your debt load hinders your credit score. And when your credit score is hindered, you pay more and have less for wealth building.

As a voting citizen, I do think something should be done about state schools raising their cost higher than the rate of inflation and wage rates. I agree this issue should be addressed along with teaching personal finance. But back to how this affects your credit score. When you graduate with the debt payment and you start taking on more debt to live (because you never learned how to do a personal budget), all this debt wreaks havoc on your credit score. There are adults who have six-figure-income households who can't even afford to purchase their first home because their debt-to-income ratio is too high. Why? Because it started with that darn student loan. Now you have a couple with a combined student loan debt of over $60,000, car loans, and credit card debt trying to buy a house. It won't happen, because they never learned way back in high school the simple lessons of budgeting, debt, and how all of this will affect your credit.

Creating your financial road map for life starts early. We have options that will give us control over how bumpy and curvy the road will be. I've preached—yes, preached—to my children that Mommy and Daddy are not taking money from our retirements to pay for college. If they want to go to college, their job is to make the grades, study, and prep so they can apply for scholarships. I will help them financially (not all parents have this option), but I will not go broke trying. I've discussed what an average salary looks like for a recent college grad and what they should expect to pay to run a household. I'm proud of my son (he's the first one to go to college). He said, "Mom, I'm determined not to come out of school with a ton of student loan debt. I have a plan." He shared with me his plan. As a parent, that's what we want—for our children to have a plan and eventually function as adults and not live off of us. Right? The lessons start at home. We set examples, and they watch us. I show my children that I have line items in my budget for some of their expenses. They then ask how much money is left in their budgets. I'm hoping what they see will become a transferred behavior in adulthood.

Generational Curse

This credit thing is deep and can be a generational curse if you don't break it. I've spoken to so many women who have shared that they weren't taught how to budget or handle money growing up. Some of the women have even shared that they now give monthly allowances to their parents because the parents never learned how to handle money and the parents can't get any credit because they never knew how to pay their bills on time. The bad spending habits of parents can become the same bad spending habits of their offspring. The foundation of good credit is learning early how to handle money and a budget. That's why I am an advocate of teaching financial literacy courses in high school. Not to mention we are living in a rapidly, ever-changing digital age. The physical exchange of cash is becoming archaic, and everyone is swiping a card in exchange for goods. Even if the card is a debit card (our new form of cash), creating responsible spending habits is important for the financial comforts of our longevity. That's why getting a handle on your credit is important.

I'm teaching my children how easy it is to get a yes to anything they want with good credit. Having a high credit score makes it even easier.

You can contribute to a generation of excellent spending habits by teaching your children the importance of credit when they are able to understand the significance of the number. A good age is when your children start working and depositing money in their own checking account and making withdrawals using their own debit card. All the lessons you taught them when they were much younger (when you made them accountable for their allowance) about saving money in their piggy banks will sink in with that first job, deposit, and in my oldest child's case, the first time he overdrew his account. Up until that point, my lessons on saving money didn't have any meaning until my son starting spending money that he earned. It was beautiful watching him make transfers to his savings account and spending what remained in his checking account. He started setting savings goals and even set a savings threshold, not allowing his account to drop below a certain limit. I told him if he were a responsible banker, it would be much easier for him later to apply for a credit card at his home bank, because they've watched how he's handled his money as a banking customer. I've made conversations about money, budgeting, and credit a norm in my household.

Mapping your course to building good credit starts young, and it doesn't happen overnight. It takes time, but it is easy if you have already had a great start before signing for your first loan or credit card. Smart, responsible young people become smart, responsible adults. They just need guidance and access to information.

NOTES

Chapter 5

Starting Out

Don't compare your beginning to someone else's middle or end.

If you don't have credit, you are not alone. According to stats from the Consumer Financial Protections Bureau, in 2015, more than fifty million American adults had no credit. Now, I am sure some people purposely want to fly under the radar and don't want any credit for fear of identity theft. Some people simply do not want to be found, so they don't open a checking account or apply for any type of credit. They live on cash! This can be pretty tricky if you are trying to navigate and have a thriving lifestyle.

Starting sooner rather than later is better.

If you don't want to be one of those people who live under a rock, it's important that you establish some credit. Starting sooner rather than later is better. The length of your credit history is one of the factors that helps boost your score. Remember, we are trying to get you in the 800+ credit score club!

Establish a Banking Relationship

One of the easiest ways to get started is establishing a relationship with your banking institution. Your bank has a record of how you handle your accounts. They want to foster strong relationships with their customers. In the world of sales, it's called selling up—selling more than one product to your customer. Banks make money off credit cards. Even if you are smart and pay your card off in full each month (which is what I want you to do), they make money from the merchant who accepts your payment when you use the card. So, starting with your bank would be a smart move.

If you don't already have a checking or savings account, now is the time to do it if you want to start establishing credit. It's time to come out from under the rock! Parents, open a savings account for your children when they are young. I established savings accounts at my local credit union for my children when they were in elementary school. When my son got his first job as a lifeguard at fifteen, we went to the credit union (the same place he had his savings account) and opened a checking account and had his paycheck automatically deposited. When he went away to college, he opened another student checking account (no assistance needed on my part because he was eighteen) at a banking institution on his school's campus.

Show Proof of Income

If a bank is going to give you an unsecured credit card, they will want to make sure you have income to make monthly payments. Your income can come in different forms. If you are older and your credit is dormant, your social security or pension income (yes, there are people who still have pensions) will suffice.

Apply for Something

Take the first steps and apply for something at the bank. They want to work with you. As I've stated, they want the relationship and want to sell you a product!

There are different types of credit cards. Just like there are student checking accounts, most banks will have credit cards for college students. If you are a college student, apply for one. You will need to be ready to apply for the card on your own because most major credit card issuers do not allow cosigners, even on their student accounts. You have to look around for an institution that will allow cosigners, and you might be hard-pressed to find a cosigner anyway because both of you would be responsible for making the payments. If you can't get the student card (because the bank said no), you could ask someone (a parent or someone close) to add you to their card as an authorized user. This can be a double-edged sword. If the person adding you as an authorized user doesn't pay their bills on time, it could hurt you. If they are great credit customers, it will help. Keep in mind that being an authorized user helps, but it doesn't have the weight of having your own credit when it comes to scoring.

If all else fails, apply for a secured credit card. This is a way to establish credit on your own. Here's how it works. You establish an account and the money you place in the account is the limit you have on the credit card. You cannot use the money in the account to pay the credit card bill. The money is used as secured collateral for the card. You cannot take the money out of the account until the credit card is paid in full or you close the account. Some banking institutions start secured credit card limits as low as $300. This is a great way to get started if other options fail. Using a secured credit card, however, should not be a permanent solution. The interest rates on the cards are usually higher and there are usually annual fees on the card (annual fees on credit cards are a pet peeve of mine). The good news is your paying habits will be reported to the credit-reporting agencies. That's what you want!

Secured loans are similar to secured credit cards. You use your own money/account as collateral to get a loan from the bank. The bank reports your paying history to the credit-reporting agencies and you establish credit. Once you have proven yourself trustworthy of handling credit with secured credit (cards or loans), apply for an unsecured card with favorable rates.

I would like to mention one other free program that is offered by Experian for people who have never owned a credit card or student loan, but who are trying to boost their credit. The program is called Experian Boost. The premise is to gather the payment history of your utilities or phone bill. You link your bank account to an Experian account and they report your on-time payments to Experian. Therein lies the drawback. Your on-time payments are only reported on Experian and not Equifax or TransUnion. If you apply for credit and the company does not pull credit from Experian, your efforts to use the boost program will be in vain because your on-time payments will go unnoticed. The other drawback is having your bank account linked to an Experian account. There have been data breaches with bureaus (I was a victim of a data breach and it is why I now have my credit frozen). I would keep my antenna up with anything pertaining to my banking information. Nonetheless, some people have had success using Experian Boost and have seen their credit score rise. Just like every dollar counts in a budget, every point counts when you are trying to raise your score and establish credit.

So, if you are willing to crawl out from under a rock and get with our digital age of using credit cards responsibly, you have a strong chance of creating credit for yourself by following the previously mentioned suggestions.

Credit-Monitoring Service

Since you are getting started establishing credit, it is important that you keep an eye on your progress. It's almost impossible to see where you want to go if you don't have markers along the way. I suggest you register with one of the free credit-report sites that are available. These sites will allow you to see your score go up, up, and away, and allow you to freely view charges that pop up on your credit that may not belong to you through identity theft. Remember, however, what I suggested in chapter 1, that you should first pay for a full credit report through www.annualcreditreport.com.

Credit is big business, so most banking institutions now offer free credit monitoring for all banking relationships. If you follow my advice, you will establish a banking relationship with a local bank and open up a checking or savings account. I am able to check my score from Equifax, Experian, and TransUnion each month because of my banking relationships and my registration with Credit Karma. Credit Karma gives me a snapshot each month of my credit score with TransUnion and Equifax, and my banking institution provides me a score from Experian data. There is usually a two-point difference between the scores. This, in part, is due to when my creditors report data to the bureaus.

A few of the more popular credit-report sites include Credit Karma, CreditWise, and Quizzle.

I say they are free, but as you know, there's no such thing as a free lunch. These sites get your data in exchange for a free credit report. They make their money through offers of credit monitoring, identity theft insurance, lost wallet protection, credit alert, etc. Credit card companies also pay to run ads to apply for their credit card. The credit-report companies will match you up with a card based on your credit. So the cost to you is testing your mental strength and not getting pulled in with all the offers. If you can remain strong and ignore all the candy dangled in your face, you will be fine. Just take the freebies and keep it moving.

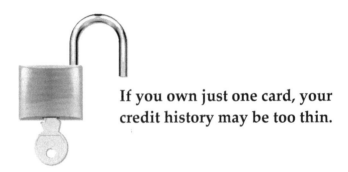

If you own just one card, your credit history may be too thin.

Apply for a Second Card

Once you've been approved for your first credit card and you've started monitoring your score with a credit-reporting service AND your score has risen to at least 700, go ahead and apply for a second card. Two is better than one! There is no hard and fast rule as to when you should apply for the second card, but I would wait at least six months. You will get a hit on your credit, because applying for the second card will be a hard inquiry. Banks and lenders check to see if you have been applying for credit all over the place, so waiting six months in between applying for cards will not look too bad. Keep in mind that hard inquiries could stay on your credit report for two years, but the initial effect of applying for credit fades in about three months, so your score will bounce back. I don't want you to be irresponsible in this process and start applying for cards all over the place. I am trying to help you build credit for larger purchases like a home for later. If you own just one card, your credit history may be too thin. Once you become a responsible credit holder, having more available credit with no balances helps your utilization rate, which I will cover later. If, by chance, you are thinking about purchasing a home, wait at least nine to twelve months before making the purchase. Mortgage lenders will look back further at your credit history.

Credit for Business Owners

Without me going any further, it is important for you to know that as a new start-up/small business owner, you are your business credit. Any business thinking about lending you money or offering you credit in your business name will look at your ability to pay back the business loan. That's why it is so important for you to work on yourself first.

There are, however, a few things you can do to make sure lenders recognize your business as legitimate. I've started four companies and never had any issues getting credit in my company name. Make sure you follow the steps listed and work on your personal credit to make it difficult for a lender to tell you no when applying for business credit:

- **Get your personal credit in order.** I think I've stressed this point ad nauseam, don't you think?
- **Form a business entity (LLC, S Corp, or C Corp).** If you haven't taken the first step in setting up a

business, then you aren't a business. You have to show proof that you have a business, so the formation of the business is important. You can do this yourself or hire an attorney for assistance. If you have the time and patience, the process is fairly easy. Go to your secretary of state's website to get started. There are other steps you may want to follow (like reserving your company name) first before setting up the company, but these are beyond the scope of this book.

- **Apply for a business EIN number.** This number is like the social security number for your business. When you open up a business bank account, you will have to supply this number.
- **Set up a Dun & Bradstreet number.** You can go to the Dun & Bradstreet website and put in your business information (Dun & Bradstreet is the business credit–reporting agency). However, you do have to be careful with this site because representatives will call you and try to sell you products to help you raise your business credit score. Don't fall for it; just put in your information. When you apply for credit for the first time, you can give them your D&B number.
- **Open up a business bank account.** Just like it is important for you to establish a banking relationship as an easier route in building credit, it is equally important for your business. I don't know if I can over-emphasize this point: do not, and I repeat, do not muddy the water and use your personal account for your business. Lend your business money and place

that money in the business account, working from the business account.

- **Set up a business phone number.** You can convert your personal phone line into a business line. I transferred an old cell number to a new carrier and had the line placed in my business name. Now when I search my old cell number, my business pops up. This is just another way for a lender to see you as a true serious business.

- **Apply for business credit in your company name.** Make sure the creditor reports to one of the bureaus (Experian, as an example). You can call the lender and ask them which bureau they report to in advance of applying for credit. If your personal credit is in order, you could use this opportunity to apply for an unsecured credit card and a line of credit in the company name. Both types of accounts will help build credit for your new business.

Now, it's time for you to do a bit of goal setting!

ACTION STEPS

1. Do you have a checking or savings account?

    _____

2. If no, what's stopping you from opening an account?

    _____

    _____

    _____

3. If yes, have you spoken to a banker to inquire about
    their credit options (credit card, secured credit card,
    secured loan)? _____

4. Did you already follow the steps outlined in chapter 1?

    _____

    If not, please go back to Action Steps in chapter 1.

NOTES

Chapter 6
Identifying the Unicorns

Don't rely on luck in your pursuit of financial freedom.

For people who have credit scores 800 and above, is it luck or intentional steps that have placed them in the 800+ credit score club? Perhaps, it is a little bit of both. Some people, like myself, just start off creating good credit habits before they even discover that their natural habits are beneficial to their credit score. So my goals for you are to make sure you employ and become cognizant of these habits now to prevent issues with your credit later. You can be purposeful and intentional with your spending, creating a great lasting high credit score.

What's so unique about individuals who have high credit scores above 800? Before I paint the profile picture of our unicorns, how many people actually fit into our unicorn category? According to data from FICO, as of April 2017, 20.7 percent of Americans have a FICO above 800! That's quite a few unicorns who are paying their loans and credit on time (since credit history makes up 35 percent of your credit score, there's a strong correlation between a high credit score and a low number of late payments).

Super-Prime Borrower

Many lenders and creditors consider what I call unicorns to be super-prime borrowers. They get the most favorable lending rates available to consumers. Here's an example of the interest rate range for new car loans. The super-prime borrower will be approved for the interest rate at the low end of the range. Check out the depth of the range!

New Car Loans

Term	APR*
Up to 12 months	2.38% to 12.28%
24 months	2.38% to 12.28%
36 months	2.38% to 12.28%
48 months	2.38% to 12.28%
60 months	2.38% to 12.28%

If we use for an example a new car costing $25,000 over forty-eight months, the super-prime borrower receiving a 2.38 percent interest rate would pay **$26,233.44** over the life of the loan. The borrower on the other end of the spectrum receiving an approval rate of 12.28 percent would pay **$31,765.92**. That's a whopping **$5,532.48** more for the same vehicle. Let's bring this example home further by looking at a TVM (time value of money) calculation on the difference. If you took the cost savings difference and tossed it in a mutual fund account getting a 7 percent rate of return, and you never add another penny to the account, after twenty years, the cost savings on the vehicle could result in an account worth **$21,408.95!**

One thing I will point out from this chart—it's easy to get a car loan, if you are willing to pay the price! Having poor credit costs you in your wallet. That's why it is so important to work on those three digits!

Now, let's delve into the characteristics of the 20 percent who are in the club.

Don't wait until you are thirty to decide to build credit and open your first account.

They got their credit in order early in life.

It takes time to build credit, and the length of your credit history is 15 percent of your credit score. When I started doing research on the profile of those who have a high credit score, I fit the profile. Getting an early start on building excellent credit is probably the luck part of the equation. As I've mentioned, when I got my first credit card in college, I wasn't thinking about my credit score. I was happy to get the credit card and knew how important it was to pay the bill on time. It was the responsible thing to do. I was not intentional on building credit at the time. My responsible behavior with payments created a direct effect on my credit. Starting the process of building credit early in my twenties helped with a strong, long credit history. My advice on creating credit history—don't wait until you are thirty to decide to build credit and open your first account. This should happen when you are in your twenties. Having a credit history longer than nine years is a plus to your score and will be important if you decide to purchase a home in your thirties.

This is why I am not a fan of personal finance professionals suggesting you don't need a credit card. Having the credit card isn't the issue as a young adult. Learning how to handle the credit when you are young is the issue. That's why I'm writing this book!

They rarely close out credit cards.

I think most young borrowers unintentionally get this wrong by thinking they are doing the right thing. Never close out a credit card. I've known people who've shared that once they paid off their credit cards, they closed them out. DO NOT DO THIS! The longer you keep the card open, the longer the credit stays in your history. This is especially important if you've used the card over the years. I checked my credit report and the oldest line item I have was established in 1994 (hopefully older than some of my readers). I'm still actively using that credit card. Six cards closed on their own due to non-usage. Here's the kicker: the card with the twenty-five-year history is not a major credit card, but a store card (don't worry, I pay the card in full when I use it because the interest rate is mind-boggling). I never closed that store card, and it has helped with the age of my credit history. Sometimes when you are offered credit on the spot when you are young, it can be beneficial later—when there is responsible usage.

They budget everything.

Those unicorns keep a budget and follow their plan, especially when it comes to adding debt payments to their budget. I consider myself an expert when it comes to budgeting. According to Malcolm Gladwell's bestseller *Outliers* (which is a great book, by the way), you need to practice a skill for ten thousand hours to make you an expert in the field (though many people have debunked this number). I do spend quite a bit of time working on my budget each month. No, it does not consume me, but I have completed a monthly budget for over thirty years. I actually enjoy paying all my bills each month and am thankful I have been able to. I'm a true planner. I think about every purchase and the impact it may have on my budget. Completing the budget doesn't mean it is perfect every month. A good budget is one where every single dollar is accounted for. Every dollar has a home (I call this zero-based budgeting). If you get to the end of the budget and there isn't enough income to cover the expenses, look for areas you can cut until the income equals the expenses. If the expenses still exceed the income after you've made cuts, then you have an income issue. It's time for you to think about creating another source of cash flow! I am as guilty as others and I have gone over my budget, but I always know where the money would come from to cover my overage. I have my money buckets to pull from (check out my first book, *One Bucket at a Time: A Woman's Guide to Creating Wealth*).

They avoid hard inquires.

If you've gone to any department store or electronic store to make a purchase, you've probably been hit with the line, "Would you like to open up an account today and save 10 percent?" If you've gone to test-drive a car and they ask, "Would you like for us to check and see how much of a loan you qualify for?", then you've been credit-hacked. In both scenarios, the sales rep pulls your credit. Every time someone pulls your credit, you get a ding on your credit, and your score—it drops a few points. This hard inquiry can stay on your credit report for two years and affect your credit score for about twelve months. It's enticing to get caught up in the discounts and the thought of saving money on the spot. The truth of the matter is you really won't save money over time, especially if you have not mastered the skills of paying off your credit in full each month. The interest rates on store credit cards are ridiculously high and will only cost you money when not paid in full each month. Avoid this hack like the plague, especially if you already have credit. This may be fine for someone who is trying to establish credit for the first time.

They don't use most of their credit.

Using every ounce of credit available to you wreaks havoc on your credit score. A lender needs to feel like you can handle what you have. When a person tells me their credit score and it's below 700, I'm usually certain it's because they are close to their credit limits. The less you use that is available to you, the better your score. At every credit workshop I've attended, everyone can recite the 30 percent rule they've heard over the years. That rule is *"Do not use more than 30 percent of the credit available to you."* That's a good rule, but not an excellent rule we unicorns follow. As of the typing of this sentence, I've only used 1 percent of my available credit. My utilization rate, like that of many people who use their credit cards for practically all purchases, changes monthly. I use my credit cards for business and to pay monthly household expenses. Because my usage is revolving, I doubt I will ever get a perfect credit score, even though I know how to get there. I would have to take a month or two and put a few things on pause with my utilization. When you have a score within striking distance of the perfect 850, you have to be strategic, and I simply don't have the energy to be that strategic since I'm already a member of the club. Most unicorns who aren't trying to be the number-one unicorn with the highest score (850) usually use less than 10 percent of their available credit.

They are obsessed with their finances.

Unicorns are obsessed with their finances. They usually can tell you outright how much they owe on their credit cards, if they have a balance at all. They know how much they have saved in their retirement accounts. This is a question I ask in every interview session with potential new clients. So many people don't know the answer to this question; they won't say or are too embarrassed. Here's a big one for the unicorns: they know their approximate net worth (assets − liabilities = net worth). Having a lot of debt keeps the unicorn up at night. They have a plan for how to pay off their debt, if they have any. All of the 800+ club members I know, including myself, find that it is important to keep a handle on their personal finances. They direct their money. They navigate their financial ship.

Does It Really Matter?

I'm sure many of you feel like you will never make it into the club and that having excellent credit is not worth the hassle. Before you start feeling sorry for yourself, the answer to this subheading is yes. It does matter and you should care. Have you ever met a person who had a vision of owning a dream home, but felt like ownership was out of reach? I have! Seeing a person go from depleted to elated when their dream finally comes true is gratifying, especially when you are able to assist with the process. Success stories of people making changes to their current circumstances to get what they want is a driving force for me.

I had a very nice woman attend one of my workshops who was well-to-do. She made a hefty six-figure salary. She had gone through a divorce a few years back and was ready to purchase her first home. Her credit had been damaged during her divorce, but she had worked hard over the years to rebuild her credit. Anyway, she came to my workshop because she could not get her credit score to move above 659. She was trying to apply for a jumbo home loan, and her current credit score was getting in the way of receiving a favorable interest rate. This was a woman who had money, but could not buy her way into receiving the rate she wanted for the loan. I shared with her a few dirty little secrets about credit, and her score went up. Here's a text message I received from her:

> Trans Union alone jumped 68 pits, you see that ?
>
> I never thought I could get the needle to move !!
>
> I wrote the baseline on 11/17, when we had lunch, it was 659 and 722 ...
>
> Your advice is working ! Smart woman !!

Receiving a message like this from her made my heart do somersaults. I was so happy for her. She got the loan and was able to move into her dream house. No, she didn't make it to the 800+ club, but she made it to the homeowners club. That's all she wanted, considering how long she had to wait after her divorce. Credit is important no matter who tells you differently. Having excellent credit keeps more money in your pocket. For those of us who like to save money, this makes a world of difference!

Now, let's see if you can incorporate a few unicorn habits in your everyday life!

ACTION STEPS

1. Do you have a budget or monthly spending plan?
   _____

   If no, what has gotten in your way of creating one?
   _____
   _____
   _____

2. Do you make minimum payments on your credit card bills each month? _____

   If yes, what is stopping you from paying extra or making the full payment?

3. What are the credit limits on your revolving accounts (credit and store cards)? _____

   A. If it is a card you haven't used in over one year, make a very small purchase on the card, then pay it off in full immediately.

4. List the credit limits for each of your credit cards. Calculate your credit usage for each card. This is done

by taking the balance amount and dividing it by the credit limit. For example, if your balance on your Visa bill is $600 and your limit is $1,500, then your credit usage is 40 percent ($600/$1,500 = 0.40). If necessary, take baby steps and first get your usage close to 30 percent, then gradually decrease your usage to the less than 10 percent range done by the unicorns. So, to calculate a 30 percent card usage, you would simply multiply your limit by 0.30, or 30 percent. Going back to our example, 30 percent of your $1,500 limit would mean your balance should never exceed $450 ($1,500 x 0.3 = $450). A unicorn would never carry a balance larger than $150 ($1,500 x 0.10 = $150).

Credit Card Name	**Balance/Limit**
1. _____	1. _____
2. _____	2. _____
3. _____	3. _____
4. _____	4. _____
5. _____	5. _____
6. _____	6. _____
7. _____	7. _____
8. _____	8. _____
9. _____	9. _____
10. _____	10. _____

Utilization Rate

1. _____   6. _____
2. _____   7. _____
3. _____   8. _____
4. _____   9. _____
5. _____   10. _____

Just remember, as your usage starts creeping over 9 percent, your score will start coming down if you are not paying your card in full each month. I'll share with you in the next chapter what you can do to fix this little problem!

NOTES

Chapter 7

What Makes Up Your Credit Score?

The whole is greater than the sum of its parts.

—Aristotle

Your credit score is like a cocktail. One missing ingredient can change the taste of the drink. If you don't have the right mix of credit, your score will be impacted. A few years ago, my husband and I decided we wanted to go ahead and pay off our mortgage. At that time, I had made the decision to leave a firm and branch out on my own. My husband was simply tired of paying the mortgage. We started out with a thirty-year mortgage and then refinanced to a fifteen-year note. Our patience was wearing thin, so we finally just paid off the mortgage (in just nineteen years). This was a huge help for me because my income had dropped and I was starting over with my new firm. It's easy not having the monthly debt of a mortgage when you have a start-up company. You would think not having the mortgage would be great for our credit. It's debt, right? And the debt is now down to zero. WRONG! My credit score dropped to the high-700 range—below 800! I lost my club status. It took several months of monitoring and playing around with the right mix of payment balances on my credit cards to regain club status. Not having the debt was a huge lesson learned on how this whole credit score game is played.

So, let's take a look at what makes up your credit score, starting with the smaller percentages first.

Credit Mix: 10 Percent

The types of credit (and the number of the different types) listed on your credit report make up 10 percent of your score and are a small fraction of the total. If you don't have all the elements in the mix, you can make it up in other areas with heavier weightings. The point of having a mix is to see your experience in handling all types of credit. Having both revolving credit (credit cards and retail accounts) and installment credit (car loans, mortgages, and finance company accounts) provides for a nice mixture of the types of credit in your report. You don't have to have one of each, so don't go and open up a bunch of credit cards. If you don't have installment credit, however, and take out a mortgage, you will see a positive impact on your credit score (you just added to the mix). When my husband and I paid off our mortgage, however, all of my installment credit went away. The payoff of the installment loan, which is paid over a designated period of time with a set number of payments, typically doesn't increase your score and should not have a huge negative impact on your score—you create a wash. In my case, however, the mortgage was the only installment loan I had (I did not have car note or student loan) and my score dropped. Thankfully, it was a slight adjustment. The good news is having a mortgage in my credit history stays on my credit report for a long time (up to ten years) and can continue to factor into my score (credit history has more weight on your score than your credit mix).

New Credit: 10 Percent

It happens to all of us. You walk into a department store to make a purchase. When you get to the counter, the cashier asks, "Would you like to save 10 percent today and apply for a store card?" Opening up several accounts over a short period of time can ding your credit score, especially for "newbies" who don't already have a long credit history. FICO takes into account how many new accounts you open and over what period of time. If you are shopping for a mortgage, auto, or student loan, FICO will provide you with a bit of grace for inquiries made in the thirty days prior to scoring and count each type within the thirty-day window as one inquiry. As an example, say you are out shopping for a car and you go to several dealerships, and they all pull your credit in a two-week period. After thirty days, FICO will only count the multiple pulls for the car loan as one.

Length of Credit History: 15 Percent

Time is on your side when you are young. That's why it's important to start early building a healthy credit history. In general, a longer credit history will increase your credit score. This is not to say you can't build good credit if you haven't been in the credit pool a long time. Everyone has a different starting point on the credit-building journey.

Paying on time and keeping those ratios low have a huge weight on your overall number. So, if you open up a store card or get approved for a student credit card at eighteen, keep the card open and continue making on-time payments. Your future self will thank you when you try to purchase your car or house.

Amounts Owed: 30 Percent

I should really ask, "Are you up to your eyeballs in debt?" This is the informal question posed by lenders when you are applying for a loan. The amount you owe creditors compared to what is available to you in credit is one of the most important factors in determining your score. The ratio of what is owed compared to what is available is your utilization ratio. For example, if you have a balance of $3,000 on one credit card and $4,000 on another credit card ($7,000 used) and each of the credit cards has a $6,000 limit ($12,000 available to you), then your utilization rate is 58 percent ($7,000/$12,000). FICO scores take into account several factors when measuring your utilization rate:

- The amount you owe on the different types of accounts you have
- The amount owed on all of your accounts (usage across all cards matters)
- If you have balances on certain types of accounts
- What percentage is still owed on your installment loan (how much of that loan is paid off)

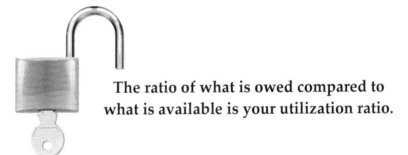

The ratio of what is owed compared to what is available is your utilization ratio.

As I mentioned earlier, people in the 800+ credit score club shine in this area because they keep their utilization rate extremely low. They don't follow the frequently quoted rule of only utilizing 30 percent of what is available to keep their current credit in good standing. In my case, I keep my utilization rate of revolving credit card limits between 1 and 9 percent. Tools like Credit Karma are extremely helpful because they allow you to keep up with your utilization rate and the balances being reported to lenders. You have more control over your utilization of credit than your mix of credit and credit history (smaller factors making up your score). Control the controllables, which means you may have to say no to yourself and resist how much you run up on your credit cards. Your resistance is important when you haven't developed the habit of paying off your balances in full each month. FICO has done extensive research and has found that people who have a swiping problem, using a high percentage of what is available to them, are more likely to have issues making some payments now or in the near future compared to people who use very little of their available credit. Resist the swipe demon that says, "You deserve this. Go ahead and treat yourself!"

Payment History: 35 Percent

Pay your bills on time—another controllable factor, and the biggest piece of the pie that makes up your credit score. Who wants to be paid late? When you loan anyone money and they say they are going to pay you back at a specified time, you expect to get your money, right? Well, creditors feel the same way. Your payment history is based on information from all the types of accounts in your report, to include major credit cards, retail accounts, and installment loans. Your pay history also includes any collections, lawsuits, liens, and judgments. Public records and collection items can also show on your report. Because your pay history has the greatest impact on your score, it's vital that you set up preventable measures to mitigate any late payments to those you owe.

Tips on Paying Your Installment Loans and Credit Card Bills

Since pay history is so important to your overall credit health, I think it's important to spend a bit more time discussing how you can be successful in this area. So below are surefire ways to help boost your score!

Set your mortgage, student loan, and car loans on automatic draft.

Late is late, and having any type of late payment will hurt you. The difference with the installment payments versus a revolving payment is how much has to be paid. If you are in a bind and can't pay your credit card bill in full, you can at least make a minimum on-time payment on the card and it will not negatively impact your credit. You cannot, however, make a partial payment on your mortgage or car note and have it not affect your credit. The terms of your loan rule. If the fixed installment payment for your car of $350 is due on the fifth of each month, well, you best pay it by the fifth of the month. Anything less than the full agreed-upon payment will negatively affect your credit score.

Besides the negative impact this has on your credit, you don't want the mortgage company breathing down your neck. Protect the roof over your head. You don't want the "repo man" taking your ride. And with regard to your student loan, if you ever wanted to negotiate loan forgiveness with student loans, having a history of on-time payments will be factored into the decision of forgiving any of your loans (there are programs that will forgive your loan if you make on-time payments for a set number of years).

Even though these items do not affect your credit if you don't pay them, consider making your car insurance payments and life insurance payments automatic as well. You can schedule when you would like for these payments to come out of your account. If you don't pay these items, the policies will just drop. You don't want to be caught by the police without car insurance, and your family would not appreciate you not having life insurance in the event of your untimely demise.

Set up text and email alerts.

When I stopped receiving paper statements in the mail, I set up alerts on my credit cards that I use frequently. The paper statements were a reminder that I needed to pay my bills. All it took, however, was for me to go to my mailbox one day and notice that a statement appeared to have been opened. This little incident pushed me to discontinue paper statements and set up the alerts. What I like about some of the alerts is they are pretty detailed, providing you with recently charged information and your total balance. The snapshots of my account balance prompt me to go online and take a deeper look at my account. You can set the payment reminders to come to your phone and pay your bill on the spot, or the reminders can be sent to your email. In either case, technology has made it easy for us to be reminded to pay our bills.

Set your payment dates to coincide with your pay schedule.

You can call any creditor and ask them to change your payment due date. If you are one of those people who is broke shortly after you're paid, this tip may be beneficial for you. You need to pay your bills before having fun (there's an exception to this rule if you have your fun money in your budget). I have one bill due two weeks after I pay myself (I like getting paid once a month). Lucky for me, I keep a budget and the money remains in my account until it's time to pay the bill. This two-week gap can be an issue for some who aren't disciplined in seeing money sit in their account before the next pay date.

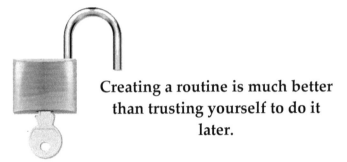

Creating a routine is much better than trusting yourself to do it later.

Select a date to sit down and pay your bills.

If you follow the step above, it will be easy for you to sit down once or twice a month and pay your bills. Leisurely paying your monthly expenses is one sure way to forget about them. Make the process a routine and select a day to work on this project. We're talking about your credit, so it should be worth you taking out a bit of time to give it your undivided attention. You can set an alert on your phone and, right from your phone, pay your bills online. Creating a routine is much better than trusting yourself to do it later. On the fifteenth of each month, I review my budget, make any tweaks, then get online and pay any bills (including my utilities) that are currently outstanding. My one installment loan comes out of my account automatically, so the only thing I have to pay are my credit cards. In my case, the due dates are toward the end of the month, so I'm pretty much ahead of the game when I make my payments.

Ask your credit card company to lower your interest rate.

If you lower your rate, you pay less in interest and ultimately get closer to wiping out the initial charge. As you decrease the balances owed on your credit cards, your utilization ratio goes down, and voila, your credit score goes up! Paying down the debt gets you closer to your goals and achieving debt-free freedom. Having astronomical 20–29 percent interest rates on credit cards doesn't get you closer to freedom. Having balances on cards with high interest rates mentally drains you because you never feel like you're making progress.

Here's what you need to do. Call up your credit card company and ask them what rate they offer their best customers. Let them know you've received offers in the mail and you would prefer working with your current carrier before transferring over your balance to another company. Do not tell them you're going to close the account (that statement makes you look like an amateur, and it hurts you because you would be closing your credit history). When they respond, ask them to lower your rate to what they offer their best customers. Now of course, this tactic will not work if you've fallen behind on your payment. But if you've been paying on time and making progress in lowering your balance, you just might get a "Yes, we will lower your rate." I offered this suggestion to attendees who came out to one of my workshops. I heard back from a few of them and received good news. One young woman shared with me that one out of three of her credit card carriers lowered her rate and she was able to get her payment due dates changed.

There really is no need to pay an annual fee on a credit card.

Carefully consider why you should be paying an annual fee on a credit card.

I am sure you're asking, "What does paying an annual fee on a credit card have to do with a credit score?" It doesn't, but having a great credit score saves you money, so I figured this is a great place to throw in this money-saving tip (I can't help myself—I love helping you save a dollar when I can!). There really is no need to pay an annual fee on a credit card. Sometimes our egos get the best of us and we feel grand pulling out a gold, platinum, or black credit card. It's a status thing, I suppose, that isn't necessary. I do not pay an annual fee on any of my credit cards, and most people shouldn't. There are plenty of cards on the market that offer perks that do not cost an annual fee. For those who do pay for a credit card, they usually don't get anything useful in exchange for the cost of the card. BUT . . . there are a few exceptions to this rule that don't apply to the majority of credit card holders:

- You are a frequent flyer and the card offers ongoing travel perks that outweigh the annual fee.
- The cashback rewards on your everyday purchases will far exceed the annual fee (there are free cashback reward cards).

- You're in the building stage of your credit and the only card available to you has an annual fee.
- The signup bonus is a sweet deal that will far exceed the annual fee (I've done this before and canceled the card before having to pay the annual fee the next year).

What If You Can't Pay Your Bill?

You're down on your luck and you simply cannot continue paying your lender. Before I give you tips on what you should consider, I would like to say this is why I do not recommend setting up automatic drafts to pay credit card bills. Sometimes things happen in your life and you simply do not have the money to pay a credit card bill. You have more negotiating power with credit card companies because the card is not tied to anything the creditor can take if you don't pay the bill. The creditor will not come to your home and take all the items you racked up on your recent shopping spree. They just want money. If you don't pay your mortgage or car payment, the mortgage company can threaten to place a lien on your home and the repo man can take your car. Just know that not paying your loan at all can wreak havoc on your credit, but if you're at this point, you are likely feeling like you're drowning, and anything will provide relief.

1. **Pick up the phone and call your lender.** Let them know what is going on with you. Lenders keep records of calls and can place a note on your account that you are experiencing financial difficulty.
2. **Negotiate a payment.** You may need to send them a spending plan showing how much you need to live on

each month and how much you can spread across each lender for a payment.

3. **Be specific about the payment you are willing to pay.** If you can only pay fifty dollars per month for two years, let them know.

4. **Hold firm with your payment offer.** Every creditor will want more money, but keep paying the agreed-upon amount. If your creditor threatens to take you to court, let them. A judge will hardly make you pay more than you can afford, especially if you are making payments.

If you cannot handle negotiating your payments, turn to a reputable nonprofit counseling service. Nonprofit counselors usually do not charge for basic budgeting services, which may be all you need so you can get yourself back on track to raising your credit score. If you are looking for a reputable nonprofit counseling service in your area, start by asking the debt-collection service of your local bank or credit union first. Falling behind on your payments will hurt your credit score, but as long as you are making payments and not charging, you may not see further damage.

The next action steps will focus on making timely payments, crucial to building credit and raising your score.

ACTION STEPS

1. Make a list of your installment loans (mortgage, car, student loans, etc.) and the due dates. Set up automatic drafts for these loans. Make sure you will have enough money in your account on the due dates to cover the payment.

    1. _____
    Payment Due Date: _____
    2. _____
    Payment Due Date: _____
    3. _____
    Payment Due Date: _____
    4. _____
    Payment Due Date: _____

2. Create the same type of list for your revolving accounts (credit card payments). Call the credit card companies and see if you can change your due dates so the payment is due closer to a pay date (when you get paid). This is only a necessary step if you run out of money before you get around to paying your bills (an unfortunate issue with those who are frequent debit card swipers and don't

follow a budget). I do not recommend having credit card payments drafted from your bank accounts. I do, however, recommend you set up alerts with each credit card company to ensure you make on-time payments. If you send in a payment on the due date, it's already late! Set the alert to make your payment far enough in advance to prevent a late payment.

3.   When are you going to pay your bills each month?

Select a day: _____

4.   Which accounts do you forget to pay each month?

   A.   Have you set an alert to make your payments?
   B.   The alerts have been set for the following accounts:

1. _____
Payment Due Date: _____
2. _____
Payment Due Date: _____
3. _____
Payment Due Date: _____
4. _____
Payment Due Date: _____

NOTES

Chapter 8
Dirty Little Secret!

Once revealed, it is no longer a secret.

I know some of you have been trying to raise your score for years. Many of you have even attended workshops, and some of you may have fallen victim to one of the many outlets who swear they can raise your score . . . "for a monthly fee." You pay them a fee, and yes, they get your score up, but they never reveal any secrets or share how you can maintain your raised score.

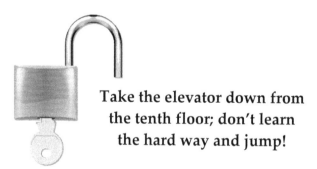

Take the elevator down from the tenth floor; don't learn the hard way and jump!

In the last chapter, I shared the importance of making on-time payments and why that is the heaviest weight to your overall credit score. But for people like myself who have, for years, consistently kept their score above 800, there are a few tricks that will help you get that score up even faster than making on-time payments. I discovered this secret by accident while I was preparing for a workshop. Experience is the best teacher, and I often share my personal life experiences with others in hopes they can learn from my lessons and mistakes. As I often say to my kids, take the elevator down from the tenth floor; don't learn the hard way and jump!

Anyway, back in October 2017, I was looking through my American Express statement, comparing it to my most recent Credit Karma report, and noticed something strange. I always pay my credit cards in full each month. The due date for this particular card was on October 28, 2017. I mentioned earlier that I sit down each month on the fifteenth and pay my bills, so paying my credit card by the fifteenth of each month ensures that the payment will arrive well before the due date on the twenty-eighth. In looking at my Credit Karma report, I noticed for the month of October I still had a balance on my account of $855, even though I had paid the card in full well before the due date. I was not a happy camper!

Having a balance showing on my credit report meant my utilization rate was 4 percent. That's no big deal, but not if you anticipated a utilization rate of 0 percent for the month of October. All this time, I had not paid much attention to this, but needless to say, the balance appearing on my FICO report piqued my curiosity. The credit card monthly statement showed a closing date of October 3, 2017. Credit Karma showed a *reporting date* of October 4, 2017, twenty-four hours after the closing date! Ah-ha! So, even with all these years of me paying my credit card in full each month, well in advance of the due date, the full payment had not been captured on my credit report. Imagine if you knew in advance how the timing of your payment could change your credit score monthly! This information would be useful if you were trying to raise your score to buy a big-ticket item like a house or a car.

My discovery took me on a treasure hunt, and I began comparing all the closing dates from my credit card statements to the reporting dates on my Credit Karma report. I found that most companies report your balance twenty-four to forty-eight hours after your closing date (it varies for each credit card), which may be twenty-one to twenty-five days in advance of the *due date*. The window between the closing date and the due date is your grace period. If you want a zero balance to show on your credit report, you need to get in front of the reporting date and make your payment BEFORE the closing date shown on your statement. Whatever the balance that is reflected on the closing date will be reported to the bureau. It is important that you remember not to make any additional charges on the card after you make the payment. Wait until the closing date before charging on the card again. You will have to play with this a few months to get the timing down. For example, when I pay my credit card bill, I am given a notice that the balance on my statement will be updated twenty-four to thirty-six hours after the payment posts. So, if I want to show a zero balance on my credit card to ensure it is reported as zero on my credit report, I need to make the payment at least *thirty-six hours in advance of my closing date.* Your closing date is pretty consistent each month and is the key to this payment strategy. You want your balance to be as low as possible when your statement closes out. That will be the balance reported to the bureaus!

Did I just confuse you with all the date terms? I imagine the explanation of all the dates can cause brain fog. Let's break down the meaning of the three dates that come in handy when you are trying to be strategic in raising your credit score while paying down debt:

- **Due Date:** This is the easy one. Your payment must be in to your creditor by this date. They want their money on the due date, which means that it needs to be sent prior to this date.
- **Closing Date:** This is the last day of the billing cycle. Your grace period falls between the closing date and the due date.
- **Reporting Date:** This is when your creditor reports the balance on your account to the bureaus. This is usually twenty-four to thirty-six hours after the closing date. The reporting date varies for each account, so you will need to monitor this date to see if it is consistent or varies monthly. You can find the reporting dates on your credit bureau report for each account listed. You can also call your credit card company and ask when they report to the bureaus.

You know this means you have a homework assignment! If you have been making payments and getting nowhere (your score has not changed), this could be the reason why. You're making payments, but by the time the interest kicks in, what is reported doesn't register as a dent in your utilization rate. I had a client who was trying to purchase a home using this method to raise her score. The strategy worked! Her credit score jumped over sixty-eight points because of timing with her payments. Now it's your turn to figure this out.

ACTION STEPS

1. What are the closing and reporting dates for each of your credit cards?

Type of Card	Closing Date
1. _____	1. _____
2. _____	2. _____
3. _____	3. _____
4. _____	4. _____
5. _____	5. _____
6. _____	6. _____
7. _____	7. _____
8. _____	8. _____
9. _____	9. _____
10. _____	10. _____

Reporting Date

1. _____   6. _____

2. _____   7. _____

3. _____   8. _____

4. _____   9. _____

5. _____   10. _____

Remember, your goal will be to make your payment before the closing date. The closing date balance will then be reported. Good luck!

NOTES

Chapter 9

Improving Your Score Beyond Payment Timing

Going that extra mile yields higher results.

I hope by now you are getting motivated and ready to change your credit score. Who needs to pay someone a monthly fee when there are endless options to undertake the task on your own? Well, I am ready to share a few more secrets. Think about it—if paying your bills on time was the key to getting an 800+ credit score, we would have far more unicorns in the club! Let's add a little icing on all the secrets I've shared with you. I can't wait until you put everything into action and reap the benefits of club membership!

Keep debt levels low compared to income.

When you apply for credit, you have to share your income. Lenders examine how much debt you are carrying and compare that to your monthly income. This measurement is called your debt-to-income ratio and is a strong barometer of your financial health. You should aim for a 36 percent or less debt-to-income ratio. Having a ratio at this level gives you wiggle room and will likely allow you to have extra money available each month to make additional payments on debt. Most members of the 800+ credit score club keep this ratio low, because they seldom use all of the credit available to them, which results in paying out less each month.

Here's the formula for calculating your DTI ratio:

Monthly Housing Costs (P+I+T+I) +
All Other Recurring Debt Payments
_____
Monthly Gross Income

*P+I+T+I (Principle + Interest + Taxes + Insurance on a mortgage)

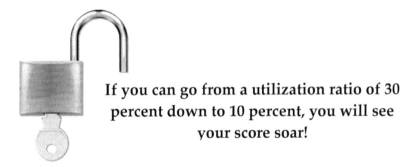

If you can go from a utilization ratio of 30 percent down to 10 percent, you will see your score soar!

Use less than 30 percent of your available credit.

I've discussed the importance of keeping your utilization rate low. As a reminder, to get that score up, you want to get that utilization ratio under 10 percent. If you can go from a utilization ratio of 30 percent down to 10 percent, you will see your score soar!

Spread charges over multiple cards.

Sometimes this works and sometimes it doesn't. It depends on the credit-scoring model and what they review. Some models look at your overall credit utilization and/or measure the utilization for each credit card. Models change over time. But in a perfect situation, this would help. Using multiple cards to spread out your debt results in multiple accounts with low credit utilization rather than one account with high utilization. Say, hypothetically, if you needed to make a $1,000 purchase. If you place that purchase on one credit card that has a limit of $2,000, that puts your utilization rate at 50 percent ($1,000/$2,000 = 0.50). If you had another credit card with a $2,000 limit, you could place $500 on each card, bringing the utilization ratio for each card down to 25 percent ($500/$2,000 = 0.25). Spreading out the charge brings your available limit down to $1,000/$4,000 = 25%. So in the event you need to make a big purchase, I would wager on spreading out the charge so you don't max out one card. But don't forget, even with all this, you would still owe $1,000!

Pay your credit card in full before the closing date.

I covered why this is important in the last chapter. To help with this step and ensure the balance is paid in full or down before the closing date, make multiple payments on your credit card each month. Even though I shared with you that I sit down on the fifteenth of each month to pay all my bills, there is no hard-cut rule that you should only pay your bills once a month. Your goal should be to get the balance down before the closing date. So, if that means you make two or even three payments a month, then so be it. It's so easy to pay from your phone. I can recall making a charge on a card to get a discount, and as soon as I got to my car, I pulled out my phone and paid the balance off. The charge will register on the card, but my payment got in front of the closing date.

Don't apply for multiple cards over a short period of time.

This could make you look unstable and a risk to creditors. Lenders fear that if you are applying for credit everywhere over a short period of time, you may run up the credit and they will have less of a chance of getting their money back.

When it comes to credit, old age is a good thing.

Don't close old credit cards.

That very first department store card you were approved for that you charged up to the limit on a shopping spree could benefit you later. Your credit history accounts for 15 percent of your credit score, so keep that old card open—don't close it! When it comes to credit, old age is a good thing. The oldest card I have in my possession is a Macy's department store card. Having that card gives me a credit age that stretches over thirty years. If you are paying off your credit and have vowed to cut them up (but not close them out), don't butcher the oldest card. Keep it, and on occasion, charge something on the card then turn around and pay it off.

Don't be surprised if your credit score drops when you pay off your student loan or mortgage that you've had close to thirty years (I shared what happened to me when we paid off our mortgage). When these old accounts fall off your credit report, your score drops because you no longer carry the history that comes with these accounts. The good news about paying off a mortgage, however, is you will have a record that you were able to carry and pay off a mortgage loan.

Avoid opening store cards for the one-time discount.

Sometimes you say yes to an offer on impulse. You're not

thinking logically, and the only thing you hear is, "10 percent discount." The thought of getting an additional 10 percent off your purchase is music to your ears. First of all, 10 percent is a little more than the tax on your purchase, and that depends on the state you reside in. In the long run, accepting the discount and opening another credit card will be chaotic to your credit, especially if you're saying yes every time you are extended the offer. When you say yes, you are creating another hard inquiry on your credit, which will lower your score. Remember, the goal is to increase your score.

Mix up the types of credit.

Having a variety of different types of credits is helpful, but by no means do I want you to go out and apply for different types of credit for the sake of having it. That will come with time. You can build your credit responsibly so that when the time comes to add on a different type of credit, your score will warrant you a good rate. Before I ever purchased my first car, I had that first credit card and on-time student loan payments. When I purchased the car, I had a history that included a complete picture of credit (revolving and installment). Throughout your lifetime, you may take out loans or utilize credit cards. You want to be prepared when the time comes by being the best borrower. I don't like the sound of being a good borrower, but that is essentially what building credit is—being a good borrower—and that is okay. I like to think of it as being a strategic borrower, because your goal is to pay credit card bills in full each month.

Ask for a credit line increase on your existing credit.

The strategy behind this move is to help with your utilization ratio. If you have more available credit with low or no balances, your utilization ratio will be low versus having less available credit with balances. If you've been paying on time and in full each month and you see that your score is rising, call your credit company and ask them to raise your credit limit. This may be a hard inquiry on your credit, so before requesting a credit limit increase, ask the credit card company if they will initiate an inquiry. If the answer is yes, just know that you will have a temporary hit. Your credit will bounce back in a few months.

* * *

There are so many action steps you can take to improve your score. I would suggest you not try tackling all these steps at once. The goal is to become a responsible borrower who knows how to handle credit. In my opinion, the first thing to get under your belt with comfort and ease is paying that credit card bill in full each month. This requires you to stick with your budget and only charge what is within your budget. Paying your credit card in full each month is one of the top key strategies I listed, and is something unicorns do regularly.

ACTION STEPS

1. What's in your wallet? What cards do you carry around daily?

   A. _____

   B. _____

   C. _____

   D. _____

   E. _____

2. From the list above, which card have you held the longest (your oldest card)? _____

3. Decide which card you listed will be your everyday credit card that will be paid in full each month. If you are working on paying off your credit cards, remove the remaining cards except for the oldest one.

Chapter 10

Signs You Are Spiraling Out of Control

Sometimes a loss can be the fuel you need for your next win.

We are ten chapters in, and I hope you have been working and implementing the action steps designed to help raise your credit score. Some of you, however, may still feel a bit of anxiety because you may be spiraling out of control with your debt. One-on-one coaching may be needed. My book was designed for the do-it-yourself type who feels like they can handle their own financial situation and pull themselves up by their bootstraps. I do, however, realize not everyone has gotten to that point. Facing yourself in the mirror can be real scary, especially if you think you are nowhere near in shape to raise your score. You may have hit rock bottom. I purposely waited to discuss this type of situation toward the end of the book because I have hope and confidence in you!

Here is a list of twenty reasons why you may be spiraling out of credit control and need a bit of assistance. A few of the examples below may be the root cause of why you are in trouble and can't dig your way up to the top of the credit score ladder:

1. You can't afford to pay your monthly charge balance in full.

2. It's a stretch for you to pay the minimum payment on your credit card each month.
3. Not only can you not pay your credit card bill, but you're also having a difficult time paying your basic living expenses.
4. Your debt is rising faster than your monthly income can handle.
5. You receive overdraft notices from your bank.
6. You wake up in the middle of the night thinking about money and how you're going to get out of debt.
7. Most of the things you've bought on your credit card were impulsive buys that you don't like or need.
8. You avoid opening any envelope you think is a bill.
9. You haven't been able to save a dollar to your emergency fund.
10. You've taken out cash advances on your credit card to buy basic necessities like food or to pay your rent.
11. You get turned down for more credit.
12. You take cash advances on one card to pay the bill of another card.
13. You paid off your credit cards with a debt consolidation loan and now the cards are charged back up to the limit.
14. You make partial payments on your loans.
15. You fall behind on the payments as soon as you open the account.
16. You've had to borrow money from a coworker until your next pay day.
17. You're an adult and you've had to go to your parents for money to pay your bills and you have a full-time job.
18. Unopened daily deliveries are stacked on your dining room table.

19. Your sugar fix is a shopping spree.
20. You have bill collectors demanding payments immediately.

Look at this list as a pop quiz. If you can identify with quite a few of the scenarios, you need to get a handle on yourself and start digging yourself out of this hole. There is always a last resort— *BANKRUPTCY.*

I hesitate to discuss bankruptcy, but I realize it's part of life and some people have no choice but to file. Before I share what I know about bankruptcy and debt, I am disclosing that I am not an attorney and you should direct your questions to an attorney if you feel like your back is up against the wall. I would imagine it's painful and humiliating if you find yourself thinking about bankruptcy. Sometimes, this is the only way out, especially if you are drowning in uninsured medical bills, consumer debt, and no income.

It is what it is! I had a dear close relative who would forgo medical care because of the cost. They unfortunately waited until they were extremely ill before getting medical attention. Sadly, they are no longer with me. Your life is far more important than a medical bill. Bankruptcy is designed to give yourself a second chance.

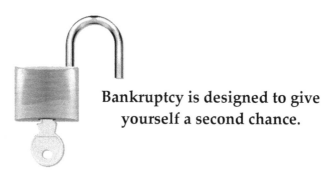

Bankruptcy is designed to give yourself a second chance.

Before you go completely broke exhausting your retirement accounts, your children's 529 plans, and mortgaging your house, go and speak with a reputable attorney. Certain items can be protected from bankruptcy. If you find yourself in this situation, not because of medical bills, but because you simply could not stop swiping (your credit card), I would suggest you seek counseling first. You may be a shopaholic. A counselor can help you figure out what triggers your spending behavior, which results in you drowning in debt. Filing bankruptcy will not help a shopaholic if you don't get to the root of your problem. Not figuring out your spending triggers will lead you back to your mountain of debt once expunged through bankruptcy.

When it comes to bankruptcy and wiping out debt, most people will file a Chapter 7 or a Chapter 13. Chapter 7 is the preferred method by most people because you wipe out most of the consumer debt, there's no repayment of the debt, and the process is relatively quick. I know I made that process sound easy and enticing (it's not). You still have to qualify for a Chapter 7 filing and some things can't be wiped away, like student loans (sorry), unpaid child support, and recent taxes.

Chapter 13 is a repayment plan, on the other hand, and most people don't want to repay the debt. In a Chapter 13 filing, any disposable income you have must be paid to your creditors for three to five years. Disposable income is any remaining money you have after subtracting allowed bankruptcy expenses.

I'm going to leave the bankruptcy conversation right here, because I really don't want this to be your option. It takes years to recover from bankruptcy. You would be better off putting in the work to raise your score.

ACTION STEPS

1. How many of the twenty situations from this chapter's list could you identify with? _____

2. Answer why to each of the situations you have identified from the list.

_____

_____

_____

_____

_____

_____

_____

_____

_____

_____

_____

_____

_____

_____

_____

_____

_____

_____

_____

_____

Chapter 11

Update on FICO

Change is inevitable—go with it.

Just when you get the hang of something, change happens. By the time this book is released, FICO will have unveiled its latest model, FICO Score 10. I waited to include this update at the end of the book because all the techniques discussed still apply and will help you raise your score. The strategies I have provided are the fundamentals needed to evolve into an 800+ credit score club member. However, the new model will benefit some and hurt others. I personally believe the new model was designed to protect lenders. It seems consumers can never get a break. Every time we find a way to benefit consumers in this debt race, lenders and technology developers change the rules of the game. For those who are CASH IS KING proponents, I am sure they are saying, "I told you so." I say to them, it is still important to learn how to be a responsible borrower. I seriously doubt I would be in the financial position I am today if I had to pay cash for everything I've accumulated, including a paid-off mortgage! Having excellent credit has expedited my net worth.

The newest version of the FICO credit score takes a broader view of how you manage debt and will raise as many scores as it will lower. Normally, bureaus take a monthly snapshot of your behavior, and if you have the cash flow to do so, you change your score monthly. Say, hypothetically, you are trying to buy a house. Before, you could wipe out all your debt right before you apply for a home loan and stay in the "no debt" holding pattern until approved, keeping the balance low or at zero until closing. FICO has gotten hip to this technique and will now peer into your financial habits for the past twenty-four months and determine if you are a risky borrower based on that past history. In my opinion, this helps the lender and allows them to charge you more in fees, by way of a higher interest rate, if your twenty-four-month history includes late payments. That's why it is imperative that you follow the habitual payment steps outlined in previous chapters. If you are starting out, you can create a flawless payment history.

Lenders have seen an increase in personal loans used to pay off credit card debt, so the new FICO model will address personal loans differently than in the past. The new scoring model looks at trended data over the past twenty-four months versus snapshots of the previous month. For people who have created excellent paying habits over a twenty-four-month period, they will likely see a rise in their score. For those who have just begun the road to great borrowing habits, it may take you some time to see a rise in your score. Past risky behavior will lower your score.

How do we make lemonade out of these lemons?

Because past regulations and settlements for tax liens, judgments, and medical collections have been in favor of consumers, the scoring models are now heavily weighted in other attributes that haven't changed for consumers. Yes, they have found a way to get you one way or another. As I stated, this protects the lender because they have a better gauge of who will be a more responsible long-term borrower. How do we make lemonade out of these lemons? We look at this new step FICO has taken as a realization that if we are going to operate in this world on credit, we need to learn to use it to our advantage, and not as a crutch to purchase things we cannot afford.

I have no idea how my credit will be affected by this new model, and neither will you, until it happens. We will have to be in "wait and see" mode. I do know I have been in the 800+ club for a very long time. Who knows? Maybe I will get to 850 without trying any of the methods I shared with you. We shall see.

ACTION STEPS

1. How do you handle change?

    _____
    _____
    _____
    _____
    _____
    _____
    _____
    _____
    _____
    _____
    _____

2. Are you willing to put in the extra work needed to raise
    your credit score? _____

3. What past spending habits have you been proud to implement?

_____
_____
_____
_____
_____
_____
_____
_____
_____
_____
_____

4. What past spending habits are you going to dump?

_____
_____
_____
_____
_____
_____
_____
_____
_____
_____
_____

Chapter 12

Credit Protections

Protecting the fruits of your labor is not a principle, but a necessity.

I hate to start this chapter on a sour note, but in the age of technology, if someone wants badly enough to steal your identity, they can. But, if you've worked really hard to raise your credit score, there are ways to protect it. You can lock or freeze your credit!

I was a victim of the 2017 Equifax data breach. I was taken aback when I received notice from Equifax that along with myself, nearly 150,000 other people's personal information had been exposed. Equifax agreed to a global settlement with the Federal Trade Commission, the Consumer Protection Bureau, and states to help people who were affected by the breach. That's when I froze my credit and received free credit monitoring.

As you would imagine, I was angry. My biggest fear was that someone would take my information and run up a mountain of credit card debt and I would have to prove it wasn't me. What a nightmare this could have been. Luckily for me, I was informed in time to freeze my credit. Credit freezes and credit locks help protect all your hard work in raising your score. Both techniques make it more difficult for anyone, including lenders, to pull your credit or open an account in your name. This entire debacle opened Pandora's box with vendors trying to sell me products to lock my credit.

Credit freezes and credit locks help protect all your hard work in raising your score.

I am a stronger proponent of credit freezes than credit locks for the following reasons:

- Credit locks can cost you more and possibly come with a monthly fee.
- Credit freezes are regulated by federal law.
- Unfreezing your credit takes more work because a PIN code is required for each bureau, which can be a hassle if you are tempted to open more credit.

I discovered the power of a credit freeze with employers when I was applying to become an insurance broker with a carrier. The insurance company informed me that in order to write their product, I had to temporarily unfreeze my credit so they could take a peek at my credit history. They requested a twenty-four-hour thaw. Mind you, I was not applying for credit, but applying to be a contractor for a company. This is another argument that having poor credit can possibly ruin your chances of employment. I also had to temporarily unfreeze my credit when I purchased a car after driving my SUV for eleven years. Unfreezing your credit can be a hassle, but in a good way. You mentally have a cooling-off period and have time to think whether the purchase is worth the hassle of the credit thaw.

What I love about credit freezes and locks is they prevent creditors and lenders from accessing your credit history. If an identity thief gets their hands on your personal information and social security number to apply for anything like a credit card, car, mortgage, etc., the creditor would turn down the application because they can't access the information. In my case, because I've set up alerts, I would also be informed by Credit Karma that an attempt was made to use my personal information. Oh, if you are thinking about using a service like Credit Karma, Credit Sesame, or Credit-Wise to keep an eye on your credit, you will need to establish the accounts before setting up the credit freeze or lock. The good news is having a credit freeze on your account does not impact your credit score, so you are still able to regularly check to see if that score is rising. Because a credit freeze, unlike a credit lock, is federally regulated, if a thief fraudulently accesses your credit file while you have a freeze on your files, you will have better liability protection under state law. The federal law regulates credit freezes.

How to Set Up a Credit Freeze

In order to fully protect your credit, you will need to initiate a freeze with each of the three major credit reporting agencies: Equifax, TransUnion, and Experian. I went directly to each of the websites of the bureaus and they provided online instructions to set up the freeze. At the time of me freezing my credit, there was a small three-dollar fee to set up the service. Now, freezing and unfreezing your credit is free, thanks to the Economic Growth, Regulatory Relief, and Consumer Protection Act. Here are the website addresses and phone numbers for each of the bureaus:

- Experian: www.experian.com/freeze/center.html, 888-EXPERIAN (888-397-3742)
- Equifax: www.equifax.com/personal/credit-report-services/credit-freeze, 800-349-9960
- TransUnion: www.transunion.com/credit-freeze, 888-909-8872

How to Thaw Your Credit

The hassle of thawing your credit is probably why credit locks are so popular. Once you set up the freeze, you need a PIN code to thaw each credit file. Requesting the thaw doesn't take long, however. You can request a permanent or temporary lift on your credit online or by phone, and according to the Federal Trade Commission, the bureaus have one hour to lift a freeze (if your request is made by phone or online). When I was applying for a car loan, I temporarily unfroze my credit and told the dealership they had forty-eight hours to get what they needed before the freeze went back on my file.

How Credit Locks Are Different

Credit locks, like credit freezes, protect your credit from criminals. The major difference is how you unlock the credit. With a credit lock, you activate and inactivate the freeze on your credit online or through an app, typically using a username and password. You enter into a contract with a bureau (the contract is not federally regulated like a freeze) with credit locks and it could cost you an ongoing monthly fee, which could get a little pricey over time. Some of the bureaus will lock your credit for free, so check with each.

In addition to freezing and locking your credit, set up alerts on your accounts with your credit card companies to notify you if large charges are coming across your account. You can also set alerts with the free credit report companies like Credit Karma, to alert you if someone is trying to use your credit. If your credit is frozen, however, you don't have to worry about someone opening an account in your name.

ACTION STEPS

1. Do you have enough established revolving credit (credit cards)?

2. Are you able to keep your utilization ratio below 10 percent each month even when you charge on your accounts?

If you have enough established revolving credit and you are not planning on applying for any type of installment loans in the very near future, go ahead and freeze your credit with each of the credit bureaus. Here's the contact information for each of the credit-reporting agencies:

Experian	1-888- EXPERIAN (1-888-397-3742)	Experian Security Freeze P.O. Box 95554 Allen, TX 75013
Equifax	1-800-349-9960	Equifax Information Services, LLC P.O. Box 105788 Atlanta, GA 30348

TransUnion   1-888-909-8872   TransUnion LLC
P.O. Box 2000
Chester, PA 19016

Once you freeze your credit, don't forget to place your PIN codes for each of the credit-reporting agencies in a safe place!

Epilogue

Technology Has Changed the Rules of the Game

Even if you decide to remain on the sidelines, learn the rules from those who have mastered the game.

I am aware that there are many rules of thought on the subject of credit. Some people believe credit isn't necessary and using cash is the way to go. This is a protective mechanism for many. It keeps them off the grid and away from cyber criminals. Old-schoolers believe paying with cash keeps you out of debt—this is true. Navigating life this way, however, can be an inconvenience. In my opinion, not evolving with the times can have a crippling effect on your life. I know this firsthand because I have family and friends who live a cash-only lifestyle. Their road to wealth-building has been a slow one.

Innovation is great, and we should try to adapt. That includes how we transact. Technology has changed our lives for centuries. When was the last time you used a pay phone? My point exactly. (Some of you reading this do not have a clue of what a pay phone looks like. The closest you will ever get to a pay phone is viewing one in a museum—I digress). The way we spend money should be no different. We should adapt to technology, helping us smoothly transition forward in life. The key to winning with technology is learning the rules of the game. When you learn the rules, you can toggle back and forth in both worlds, not being crippled by staying on the sidelines of only knowing one way of doing anything.

Many consumers have been crippled because they do not know how credit works. They are drowning in debt and can't get ahead because they were never taught how to use credit. Running away from the matter by avoiding credit and only using cash doesn't help. Having good credit is an excellent leveraging tool for wealth-building. I am a homeowner because of my credit, and not because I had all the cash initially to pay for my home. Very little cash was used for the down payment to purchase my first home at the age of twenty-six. I leveraged my credit and ultimately made money when I sold the house and purchased a second one.

Personal finance is a life skill everyone should learn. Whose responsibility is it to teach this life skill? I think personal finance courses should be mandated in high schools well before a child can get approved for a credit card or sign off on a student loan. My husband (who's a former educator) and I had a debate about the subject of personal finance in the school system, and he said the school systems do not have funding to add another mandated course. I believe our states and governments can find funding for whatever they think is important. This subject is important!

If parents aren't versed in personal finance, they can't teach their children; that's why the subject should be a mandate. The first time most students are faced with a debt decision is when they apply for a college loan. Even then, no one discusses the ramifications of accepting the loan. How ironic is it in our country that a student can get approved for a $50,000 student loan, with no worries from the lender of paying back the loan, but that same person can't be approved for a $50,000 business loan without having decent credit? Yes, we have a credit crisis in this country, but the crisis goes far beyond our lack of self-control with spending.

The crisis is our lack of knowledge. Information and access to capital fuels innovation and can close the wealth gap. Without knowledge and information, we perish!

How do you defend yourself from the temptations of credit when you are never taught how to use it? Saying no to credit is just as difficult as saying yes to a cash-only life. Both lifestyles take discipline. It requires discipline to save cash for everything just as it takes discipline to only charge what you can afford to pay for in full each month. We are moving closer to a cashless society. We see this more and more each day with all the new ways to transact and exchange money.

One of the fastest ways to create wealth in this country is through real estate. One of the easiest ways to purchase real estate is using your good credit. Lenders appreciate good borrowers. Yes, you are indebted to the lender, but you get something in exchange without using your own money. Everyone wins! Credit isn't the enemy; our lack of knowledge is the villain. Learn how to leverage credit to your advantage and you, too, can live the life of your dreams.

Your Credit after the
Great Pause of the COVID-19 Pandemic

I started writing this book during a thriving economy, then the country froze because of the pandemic of COVID-19. It seems like overnight, everyone in the world became a technology expert. We took the time to learn how to operate work-from-home technology and other virtual software. We paused to survive. We learned a new skill.

Understanding how credit works could be your new skill. The other side of this "Great Pause" will not look pretty for many when it comes to their credit. People who didn't have an emergency funds will rely heavily on credit to get by until they can resume life again, work again, open their business again. Those who are members of the 800+ club will be far better off than those who are not or those who don't have cash.

Remember the new car I mentioned in the first half of my book? Well, I refinanced the loan during this pause to less than 2 percent (1.98 percent on a used car loan is excellent and only offered to the best credit customers). Money has become cheap and will likely be so for a long time. For those who have good credit, refinancing old loans will be money in the bank for you.

Take the time out of your life and learn all about credit. Make it a goal to raise your score. Use credit as a leveraging tool and become a member of the club—the 800+ Credit Score Club!

Appendix
Debt Ratios

Consumer debt payments should not exceed **20** percent of NET income

- **Housing debt** should be less than or equal to **28 percent of gross income**
- Housing plus all other recurring debt should be less than or equal to **36 percent of gross income**

Housing: 28% Ratio

$$\frac{\text{Monthly Housing Cost (P+I+T+I) **}}{\text{Monthly Gross Income}}$$

Housing and All Other Debt Ratio: 36% Ratio

$$\frac{\text{Monthly Housing Costs (P+I+T+I) +}}{\text{All Other Recurring Debt Payments}}$$

$$\text{Monthly Gross Income}$$

** P+I+T+I (Principle+ Interest + Taxes +Insurance)

Emergency Fund

- 3–6 (6–9) months in nondiscretionary expenses in an emergency fund
- Nondiscretionary expenses include only those expenses that do not go away if you lose your job, such as mortgage, utilities, food, car loan, property taxes, and insurance premiums
- Nondiscretionary expenses do not include income taxes, payroll taxes, and contributions to a retirement savings account.

Bibliography

"29 Credit Score Statistics for 2019." *Lexington Law*. December 30, 2018. https://www.lexingtonlaw.com/blog/finance/credit-score-statistics-2018.html."

Center for Responsible Lending, The Leadership Conference Education Fund, NAACP, National Urban League, and UnidosUS. *Quicksand: Borrowers of Color and the Student Debt Crisis*. N.p.: CRL, LCEF, NAACP, NUL, UnidosUS, 2019. https://www.responsiblelending. org/sites/default/files/nodes/files/research-publication/crl-quicksand-student-debt-crisis-jul2019.pdf.

CFPB Office of Research. *Data Point: Credit Invisibles*. Washington, DC: Consumer Financial Protection Bureau, 2015. https://files.consumerfinance.gov/f/201505_cfpb_data-point-credit-invisibles. pdf.

Cororaton, Scholastica (Gay). "All-Cash Sales: 23 Percent of Residential Sales in January 2017." National Association of Realtors. March 2, 2017. https://www.nar.realtor/blogs/economists-outlook/all-cash-sales-23-percent-of-residential-sales-in-january-2017.

Daly, Lyle. "Here's How 6 Credit Card Applications in 1 Day Affected My Credit Score." *The Motley Fool*. January 2, 2019. https://www.fool.com/the-ascent/credit-cards/articles/heres-how-6-credit-card-applications-in-1-day-affected-my-credit-score/.

Federate. "College: The New 'Debt Sentence.'" *Envestnet Institute*.

September 18, 2019. https://www.envestnetinstitute.com/article/college-new-debt-sentence.

Gladwell, Maxwell. *Outliers: The Story of Success.* New York: Little Brown and Company, 2008.

Herron, Janna. "How New FICO Changes May Lower—Or Boost—Your Credit Score." *Yahoo Money.* January 23, 2020. https://money.yahoo.com/fico-credit-score-change-210252419.html.

Equifax. "Place or Manage a Freeze." Accessed January 5, 2020. https://www.equifax.com/personal/credit-report-services/credit-freeze/.

Experian. "Security Freeze." Accessed January 5, 2020. https:// www.experian.com/freeze/center.html.

Federated. "College: The New 'Debt Sentence.'" Envestnet Institute. September 18, 2019. https://www.envestnetinstitute.com/article/college-new-debt-sentence.

Irby, LaToya. "The 800 Credit Score: What It Means and How to Get One." *The Balance.* Updated April 14, 2020. https://www.thebalance.com/what-does-an-800-credit-score-mean-4156928.

Kagan, Julia. "Fair Credit Reporting Act (FCRA)." *Doctor Of Credit.* June 25, 2019. Updated May 2, 2020. https://www. investopedia.com/terms/f/fair-credit-reporting-act-fcra.asp.

Loftsgordon, Amy. "What's the Difference between a Credit Freeze and a Credit Lock?" *Nolo.* February 16, 2020. https://www.nolo.com/legal-encyclopedia/what-s-the-difference-between-a-credit-freeze-and-a-credit-lock.html.

Money Tips. "Many Americans Don't Know Their Credit Score." *Atlanta Journal-Constitution.* June 24, 2019. https://www.ajc.com/business/consumer-advice/many-americans-don-know-their-credit-score/KOsscIGzSl2oY1wu4QlpXL/.

NAR Research Group. *REALTORS Confidence Index Survey.* Washington, DC: National Association of Realtors, 2020.

https://www.nar.realtor/sites/default/files/documents/2020-03-realtors-confidence-index-04-17-2020.pdf.

O'Neil, Cara. "When Chapter 7 Bankruptcy Is Better Than Chapter 13 Bankruptcy." *Nolo*. February 11, 2020. https://www.nolo.com/legal-encyclopedia/chapter-7-vs-13-bankruptcy-29834.html.

Smith, Sandy. "Credit Repair Services Can Be Scams." March 4, 2019. https://yesiamcheap.com/credit-repair-services-can-be-scams/.

Stolba, Stefan Lembo. "What Is the Average Credit Score in the U.S.?" Experian. September 4, 2019. https://www.experian.com/blogs/ask-experian/what-is-the-average-credit-score-in-the-u-s/.

Szmigiera, M. "Value of debt owned by consumers in the U.S. 2019, by type." Statista. December 19, 2019. https://www.statista.com/statistics/500814/debt-owned-by-consumers-usa-by-type/.

The Ascent Staff. "Here's What Americans' FICO Scores Look Like—How Do You Compare?" *The Motley Fool*. November 15, 2018. https://www.fool.com/the-ascent/credit-cards/articles/heres-what-americans-fico-scores-look-like-how-do/.

TransUnion. "Credit Freeze." Accessed January 5, 2020. https://www.transunion.com/credit-freeze.

About the Author

Terrell Dinkins, MBA, ChFC®, CDFA®, is a financial advisor, wealth-empowerment speaker, and author. As an advisor, she has a tremendous passion for creating intelligent financial strategies that help individuals, families, and small-business owners achieve their personal financial goals. Maximizing wealth potential and minimizing costs and inefficiencies are key goals Terrell aims for with all her clients.

She has been featured in magazines and newspapers and has spoken to numerous groups, providing expert advice on personal finance. She has traveled international waters speaking to audiences about wealth-building and wealth management. Her first book, *One Bucket at a Time: A Woman's Guild to Creating Wealth,* has received great reviews from the US Review of Books, Midwest Book Review, and readers.

Terrell has achieved the distinguished ChFC® designation from the American College of Financial Services. ChFC® designees must meet experience requirements and adhere to continuing education and ethical standards. Terrell has also obtained the CDFA® designation through the Institute for Divorce Financial Analysts.

Terrell is a true "Georgia peach," born and raised in Atlanta,

Georgia. She completed the Executive Program in Financial Planning from Terry College of Business at the University of Georgia. She earned her MBA from Mercer University in Atlanta and her BBA in finance from Georgia Southern University in Statesboro. She is a wife and mother of two children and a life member of Alpha Kappa Alpha Sorority, Incorporated.

ONE
BUCKET NATION

Follow One Bucket Nation on:

 @onebucketnation

 @onebucketnation

 @onebucketnation

Also available on:

OneBucketNation.com

CPSIA information can be obtained
at www.ICGtesting.com
Printed in the USA
LVHW080021210321
682005LV00009B/45